Copper
Moons

Copper Moons

Susan Yoder Ackerman

HERALD PRESS
Scottdale, Pennsylvania
Waterloo, Ontario

Library of Congress Cataloging-in-Publication Data
Ackerman, Susan Yoder, 1945-
    Copper moons / by Susan Yoder Ackerman.
        p.   cm.
    ISBN 0-8361-3501-5
    1. Ackerman, Susan Yoder, 1945-   . 2. Missionaries
wives—United States—Biography. 3. Missionaries wives—
Zaire—Biography. 4. Mennonites—United States—Biogra-
phy. I. Title.
BV3625.C63A32 1990
266'.97'092—dc20
[B]   89-37901
                                                     CIP

COPPER MOONS
Copyright © 1990 by Susan Yoder Ackerman. Published by
    Herald Press, Scottdale, Pa. 15683; released
    simultaneously in Canada by Herald Press,
    Waterloo, Ont. N2L 6H7. All rights reserved.
Library of Congress Catalog Card Number: 89-37901
International Standard Book Number: 0-8361-3510-5
Printed in the United States of America
Cover art by Susan K. Hunsberger
Design by Jim Butti

97 96 95 94 93 92 91 90 10 9 8 7 6 5 4 3 2 1

To my father, Lauren A. Yoder,
whose curiosity and caring
have made him welcome
in out-of-the-way places
all over the world

Contents

1. "Where's the Groom?"... 9
2. "Why Does One Marry, Anyway?"..........................21
3. The Last Place in the World 25
4. Hostage for Christian Marriage...........................36
5. The Ticking Ferns...43
6. Prisoners!...60
7. Crossing the Border...73
8. The Smoke that Thunders.....................................80
9. Wankie's Wilds...94
10. The Moon and the Matopos 103
11. Hurtling Toward Lusaka..................................... 116
12. Night of the Five Bandits................................... 126
13. Mistress of Maniema 143
14. First Fever... 154
15. Back-door Morgan.. 161
16. Shadows at Star Mine 169
17. The Dinner That Disappeared............................ 181
18. Tea in the Garden.. 189
19. Shattered! 200
20. Health and Hunger.. 218
21. Stalking the Crocodile 229
22. What Africa Chooses to Give to You 242
23. Persistently Africa... 250

The Author... 263

1
"Where's the Groom?"

There was no time for protracted good-byes that Sunday afternoon, and I was glad. Just time enough to check my bags, pay the small amount of excess baggage I might owe, and squeeze quick hugs around parents, uncles, aunts, sisters, and other well-wishers who had come out to Patrick Henry Airport to see me off. On a bench to the side of the waiting room I set the attaché case filled with books I couldn't live without and the flight bag, a trousseau gift, packed with all sorts of heavy goodies. That favorite fruit cake, for example, had not been easy to find in midsummer, but was sure to put a smile on Robby's face.

I swung my two suitcases onto the scales and waited for the verdict. I didn't mind paying a few dollars for excess—after all, these things had to last me a whole year.

"This all, miss?" the ticket agent barked.

"Yes," I answered. Then, as an afterthought, I added, "Except, of course, my hand luggage."

"Put it all on the scales," he barked again.

"This *is* all," I insisted, "except for what I'm carrying."

"That's what I said. It's all supposed to be weighed."

9

The fruit cake. The books. Maybe I could have done without *The Prophet* after all. "But, sir, when I went to Europe two years ago—"

"It all gets weighed. Regulations are to weigh everything."

"—I carried a waffle iron and a china fruit bowl back from Europe in a fishnet bag and nobody ever said anything about—"

"Miss, if you don't bring the rest of your baggage over here and put it on the scales, you will miss your plane."

"You're going to charge me for my purse?" I shrieked. He stood impassively. An engine whirred to life outside the terminal, and then another.

Outraged, I stomped over, picked up the leaden attaché case and bulging flight bag, and slung them onto his scales in a desperate fury.

"That'll be two hundred and seventeen dollars and thirty-four cents," said the man coldly.

I couldn't say a word. Shock and frustration filled me. I had deposited my last paycheck the week before. Now jobless, I thought of my bank account, down to just about enough money for a few days of camping in the African bush.

I shot the airline agent a scalding look. "Well, there goes our honeymoon," I blurted out as I scribbled the check.

For the first time, the agent paused in his officious activity and looked at me. He took in my cool traveling suit, the white roses that someone had thrust into my left hand, the array of friends and relatives grouped in the background, some of them clutching handfuls of rice. The question, "Where's the groom?" burned in his face, but the expression on my face, I'm sure, invited no questions.

10

There was a warning "ding-dong," notice that the plane was preparing to close its doors. My bags were whisked away; kisses flew here and there; I felt little pepperings of rice and some shrieks of gaiety as I raced grim-faced across the concrete and climbed into the revved-up airplane.

Through the crowded plane I bumped my way. The last seat was empty, but already wreathed with choking smoke. I wedged my flight bag—my weighty flight bag—under the seat and freed my hands to fasten the seat belt. As I did so, into my lap fell grains of rice; limp, fragrant rose petals; and little notes and cards that had been thrust into my unknowing hands in those last frantic moments. One flowered card lay open to a careful girlish script: "We'll miss you as our teacher, but we're sure your new life in Africa with Robby will be very exciting. Love, and God bless you. Your Sunday school class."

Putting my head down on my arms, I burst into tears. Through the Virginia skies, above the Chesapeake Bay, I wept. It may have been chagrin at the hard-hearted baggage agent. It may have been the thought of my parents graciously giving away a daughter in this unconventional way. It may have been the knowledge that I was flying eight thousand miles to marry someone I hadn't seen for two years. It may have been for all of those reasons, I don't know. I just wept.

"Are you okay?" The businessman beside me had stopped smoking by the time I lifted my puffy face to the sunlight streaming into the cabin of the plane. "I got you a glass of juice when the stewardess came by. Here." He handed me the tepid plastic cup.

I smiled, in spite of myself. "Thanks." Taking a sip of the slightly fermented juice, I flashed him another smile. "This is great!"

He seemed surprised. "Bet you just said good-bye to somebody special back there."

I laughed. "There is somebody special, but he's still eight thousand miles away!" I felt suddenly light and joyous. Gone were the months of deciding whether to join Robby in the Congo, or wait for him in Virginia for another year. I had resigned from my job as publicity director for Eastern Mennonite College. Packing, shopping, good-byes were over. Streaking along below and behind me were the clouds of the earth as I had known it up till now. Ahead lay the adventure, and I was ready to savor it all, starting with another sip of the tired juice.

But I had another rendezvous before the one with my fiancé. In New York, I would meet Nancy Sarco. The transatlantic flight and the twenty-four hours following, we were to share until she went on her way to Yugoslavia, and I to the Congo. Our friendship had its roots in pizza parties and college swimming lessons and basketball, but after college, it went beyond all that. She shared her family and home with me when I got a job in Harrisonburg, Virginia. And, interwoven into the golden days of picking mint in roadside mountain meadows, or munching apples and cheese by a rocky creek, was the presence of death. Nancy had been a Mennonite Central Committee Volunteer in Yugoslavia, and had come home to a diagnosis of Hodgkin's disease two years before. Johns Hopkins—the Baltimore Hospital where she had regular treatments—and the Hodgkin's disease itself became to us like two pesky old gentlemen who needed to be put in their place. Though they demanded all sorts of inconvenient attention, they were not to be catered to in the least.

One of Nancy's dreams, which old Hodgkin's and

Hopkins were not allowed to interfere with, was to return to Yugoslavia to visit the family which had become hers during her stay there. A period of remission of the disease allowed her dream to coincide with mine. So here I was, looking for her sweep of taffy hair in the crowds around the Pan Am lounge.

She was leaning back against her bag in a corner of the hall, her old yellow London Fog trench coat wrapped around her slim body in the chill of July air-conditioning. She smiled at me. "You're on your way. Robby, here we come!"

Being with Nancy brought to me, as always, a rush of good humor, of things being in perspective, of being close to reality. As we found our places in the big jet, even the story of the "stick-to-the-book" baggage agent in Newport News took on its hues of comedy, though I couldn't bring myself to reveal just how much I had had to pay.

Night had blanketed New York, but light and heat still seemed to sizzle from the concrete and steel of the vast cityscape. The black sky overhead looked cool and deep and welcoming, and as the plane trembled and then swept forward and upward, I felt myself lifting and urging my body onward with the huge machine. Nancy was not looking out of the window, but adjusting her pillow and trench coat around her.

"You don't really like flying, do you?" I asked.

"Not really. I'm just going through with it to get where I want to go." She smiled and prepared to close her eyes.

"Nancy." I didn't know how to say it when I didn't really know what it was I wanted to say. I just knew—what with old Hodgkin's and Hopkins so temperamental—I didn't want to lose this night of companionship above the Atlantic Ocean.

"I wasn't going to sleep, just trying to suspend consciousness," she said, understanding. "I can still listen."

The rich smell of hot coffee began to drift back from the galleys, and again that new feeling of well-being went through me. All around us the passengers were making themselves ready for the luxurious midnight meal and then an attempt to get some sleep to beat the jet lag they would encounter in Europe's morning.

"I can't believe I'm really doing this, Nancy," I began. "First there were all those letters. Remember how Robby wrote, asking me to join him for his third year in the Congo. It sounded romantic to me, and I wrote back, excited about it. Of course, mail takes forever, and before he had received my reply, he wrote a discouraged letter—his car had been stolen or some government officials gave him a rough time, he couldn't wait to leave, and he'd never bring me out to such a crazy place. My enthusiasm was considerably dampened. I wrote agreeing that it had been a foolish idea and I'd just forget about it. Meanwhile he received my first enthusiastic letters. . . ."

"And then he wrote saying to come, of course, right?" Nancy put in.

"Yes, but by then I had gotten so confused. I decided to end the indecision with a polite, curt little note informing him that we could resume marriage negotiations when I saw him again back home in Virginia—and not a minute before. Case closed."

"But that didn't stop him," laughed Nancy.

"No, or I guess I wouldn't be on this plane with you tonight, would I?" I laughed. "When letters fail, try ham radio. Robby quickly studied for and passed a test to get an amateur radio license. Evidently all his pilot-missionary friends had rigs he could use."

"But of course, you didn't have a radio, so how did he reach you?" Nancy asked.

"One night I got a phone call from a man in North Carolina, who said he had talked to Robby. He gave me a time and date that Robby would be on a certain frequency and told me to find myself a local amateur radio operator."

"Was that hard to do?"

"My cousin, Ray Yoder, was in high school at Eastern Mennonite and had a rig he used in the college observatory. As I walked into the radio shack, with all its wires and technical equipment, it didn't seem possible that I could talk to someone eight thousand miles away. But I had my speech ready about waiting until I saw him here in Virginia. Ray tuned up the radio. Suddenly there was Robby saying, 'Susan, I've arranged everything and am waiting for you to come.' '

"And you didn't say no after all!" laughed Nancy.

I laughed, too. "I said, 'When do you want me to come out?'! I did warn him that I would reserve a few weeks for changing my mind, if necessary, after I got there."

"I predict you won't," said Nancy soberly. "Still, I can't imagine you married. But then Bunni's been married for six months, and she's the same person as ever. I guess if I knew Robby it would seem more real. How did you know you should marry him? You haven't seen him in two years and only knew him a total of nine months before that. You're each from very different backgrounds. As Jan might ask, do you know where he stands on miracles, pacifism, shaving legs, and Nestle's selling baby formula in third world countries?"

We broke into laughter. "Jan Steiner! At least her relationships with men were never boring!" I said.

15

Our steaming trays of filet mignon and crab salad and petits fours surprised us out of our conversation. We were ready to eat. There's something strange about eating dinner miles above the earth, covering ten miles a bite or a sip. I looked at the suspended cup of fragrant coffee, the liquid barely trembling as it cut through the clouds, nothing but a sheet of metal between it and the moon.

Nancy broke into my thoughts. "But you haven't answered my question. I mean, was it love at first sight? Were you ever unsure?"

I stopped eating and was silent for a moment. Then I laughed. "It was simple. A Mickey Mouse radio in a toy shop in Brussels helped me make up my mind!"

She looked at me with a frown. "That sounds like a story I haven't heard."

"It *is* a story," I agreed.

"Well, we have all night," she reminded me. "Let's hear it."

"All right. Let's go back two years. It's the year Bunni and I came to Yugoslavia looking for you, and they had already sent you home, sick."

And so I began the story:

The summer I was twenty-one, I desperately needed a sign from heaven. Kicking up my heels in Europe with my friend Bunni, I had crossed paths (I can't honestly say by chance) with Robby Ackerman, who was studying French before Pax service in the Congo.

Being a very rational person, he convinced me of how sensible and thrifty it would be to extend my stay a few weeks and join him in his French class. After all, I'd get more value out of my transatlantic ticket that way. And I'd get a head start on my French studies back at the College of William and Mary in September.

16

But as those weeks quickly flew by and the day of parting approached, I knew I was in over my head. I needed a sign from heaven, and I needed it quick.

There was no question that we were in love. There had never been sunsets as radiant as the ones we watched from the top of the old Beffroi in Mons. There had never been castle gardens as enchanted as the ones we wandered through. There had never been picnics like those we had with only a big custard *tarte* bought at a farmhouse door on weekend bike trips.

And we had made promises to each other. Would those promises carry us through two years of separation as well as the rest of our lives? Or were we just blinded with the romance of being together in Europe?

I was still debating, when the last day of class arrived. Our classmates said good-bye to us with all the teasing and good advice that people in love always have to put up with. Our professor was intent on proving that his audiovisual method of teaching language was superior to traditional methods. He recorded a playful dialogue between Robby and me that he hoped to compare favorably with our stiff *bonjours* the opening day of class four weeks before.

The last morning in Brussels before Pan Am was to whisk us apart, we sat in Robby's fifth-floor garret room. We were trying to pin down our dreams, sharing ideas for a cabin we might someday build in a pine forest. Then the thought of hot *gaufres* presented itself as a kind of escape valve from thoughts of the far-off future. We pulled on our coats and hurried down to the street to find a corner stand which sold the yeasty, sticky waffles.

Brussels is known for its coldness, not only gloomyweatherwise, but also in the distance that human be-ings put between themselves and those that jostle them at cobblestone street corners. The round man that set little mounds of dough to await the smoking iron never met our eyes. We counted out our francs and he silently handed us the heavy, paper-wrapped waffles.

Munching, we ducked raindrops under awnings, through little shopways and alcoves, reading signs for horsemeat balls and *filet américain*—a raw hamburg-er concoction that no American I knew would have touched. There was an umbrella shop, an Oriental rug shop, and there—

We stopped. In the window of the next shop were just the knives and forks to be used in the little cab-in we had spent the morning dreaming of. Graceful stainless steel they were, with warm teakwood han-dles. I was only admiring them, but Robby began counting his traveler's checks. After all, he reasoned, a girl who didn't want a diamond ring had to have *something* concrete and beautiful.

There were still twenty minutes to wait until the shop would reopen for afternoon business. Across the street at a toy shop there was an open door where we could perhaps find shelter from the rain.

No one but the manager was inside, relaxing at his desk and listening to the midday news over a little red Mickey Mouse radio hanging rakishly from a wall display. He motioned us in.

We looked at the music boxes and the dolls and the brightly painted pull toys a little shyly, not quite far enough along with our dreams to discuss what our future children might like. The rain drummed on, and the radio jabbered its incomprehensible French news above the static.

Suddenly I heard Robby speaking—but not from my side. His voice was coming from that Mickey Mouse radio as if it were enchanted!

Whirling to look into each other's eyes, we listened in utter disbelief.

In halting French, his voice portrayed the role of a shopkeeper telling the prices of his eggs, cheese, and bread.

"And how much do I owe you?" I heard my *own* voice pipe breathlessly back, carrying on the classroom dialogue we had gone over so many times.

"Nothing, madame," his gallant voice suddenly improvised over the prescribed dialogue. "Because you have beautiful blue eyes, and I think I'm in love with you!"

There was a roar of classroom laughter and applause. Then the recording cut off and switched back to the announcer's voice. From what little my astonished ears could pick up, he was broadcasting all over Europe the remarkable success of M. Van Vlasselaar's audiovisual teaching techniques.

"That was us! *C'était nous!*" We turned upon the little manager. *"C'était nous! La radio!* It was us, talking on the radio!"

He nodded politely. I'm sure he hadn't listened to a word of that insignificant little commentary on language education that the radio station had decided to air at just that moment.

But we left the toy shop, glowing in the rain. Never had a city been so charming as Brussels; never tableware so lovely as that we went on to buy; never lovers so smiled upon by little old ladies as we. The stolid *gaufre* seller might as well have been jolly Kris Kringle as we passed him and waved a friendly greeting on our way back.

The glow has carried us through those two years of separation. I don't mean to give the Mickey Mouse radio all the credit, of course. I think it was someone who understands about signs from heaven. I can picture him arranging the stage props for his little production: a chilly rain to keep the toy shop owner in at noon, the enticement of hot waffles to get us out *in* the rain, the tempting tableware to lead us to wait in the toy shop, a disc jockey with the impulse to play the professor's tape just at the right moment, and the red plastic Mickey Mouse radio thrown in for a touch of humor.

How could I doubt any longer? If a voice in a Brussels toy shop had told me in yet another way that Robby loved me, and all Europe heard with me, I was ready to go on with the whole pleasant project for as many years as we had before us.

I finished my story and came back to Nancy curled up with her pillow and red blanket. The stewardess had removed our trays. The lights were dimmed for those who might be able to get to sleep before the sun we were rushing toward would flood the cabin again.

I grinned a little sheepishly. "Well, that's our last story. And it's two years old. But it should carry me through till—till tomorrow, I guess."

2
"Why Does One Marry, Anyway?"

I opened my eyes and frowned at the brilliant sunlight burning through the window beside me. My head ached, and I pulled down the plastic curtain to shut out the African rays. I thought to myself that we were probably directly over the equator—no wonder my head ached. Spending the night on Sabena's Boeing 707, after the previous night in Brussels when Nancy and I had giggled and talked through the night unable or unwilling to sleep, I was exhausted. It had been a long two days.

Another two hours until landing in Lubumbashi. Numbness crept over me. The time had come so close that I felt drawn into the silence of the eye of a hurricane. Behind me and before were the whirling winds.

"*Qu'est-ce que vous prenez?*" the hostess broke into my thoughts.

"Oh, *un jus d'orange, s'il vous plaît,*" I said hastily. She was just serving a glass of bubbly champagne to the young Belgian sitting beside me.

"No, no, don't give her juice!" he protested suddenly. "She's getting married in a few days. Please, pour the champagne! It is my pleasure to offer you the champagne, miss!"

21

"Thank you, but I'd really rather have the juice," I insisted.

He was incredulous and made several more attempts to overcome my reluctance. The smell of the champagne sickened me. What was I doing on this airplane far above Africa anyway?

It had been so much fun to be Susan Yoder, single, independent, and on my own. It had been especially easy to relate to men, because I had a nebulous fiancé that allowed me to enjoy their company risk-free. I was everybody's friend, and if someone expressed a wish for more than friendship, I had my regretful answer ready. It was a position of power, and I was about to trade it for something else.

When I told the fatherly professors at EMC I was going to Africa to marry a person I hadn't seen for two years, they took me aside with cautionary words. After all, nobody knew Robby. Nobody knew his family. He didn't have a Mennonite name. He came from a long line of military officers. He had also come perilously close to being kicked out of two colleges, but I wasn't about to tell the professors that. I could see the concern in their faces over coffee mugs in the faculty lounge and could imagine them saying, "Susan seemed so nice and stable. What *has* gotten into her?"

What *had* gotten into me? I knew the kind of man I had always wanted to marry. A solid, comfortable person from my own cultural tradition but not bound by it. Someone who shared my love of poetry, of reading and writing. Someone who was verbally quick and loved music and singing. A safe, secure person rooted to the charms of tidewater Virginia.

Then what in the world was I doing on this airplane on my way to marry Robby? Robby, for whom the sun was "shinning" instead of "shining" in most of his letters. Robby, who would choose a car engine over a poem any day. Robby, who could get through his favorite songs only if he got the first note low enough. Robby, who was born in Beverly Hills, California, had lived in Alaska, Germany, any number of states, and had now chosen Africa, of all places.

I reached down to open my attaché case and rummage through the stash of paperback books. Yes, here it was, *Bring Me a Unicorn* by Anne Morrow Lindbergh.[*] My eyes flew over the paragraph I had underlined:

> Apparently I am going to marry Charles Lindbergh. It must seem hysterically funny to you as it did to me, when I consider my opinions on marriage. "A safe marriage," "things in common," "liking the same things," "a quiet life," etc., etc. All those things which I am apparently going against. But they seem to have lost their meaning, or have other definitions. Isn't it funny—*why does* one marry, anyway? I didn't expect or want anything like this. I think probably that was the trouble. It must be fatal to decide on the kind of man you *don't* want to marry and the kind of life you *don't* want to lead. You determinedly turn your back on it, set out in the opposite direction—and come bang up against it, in true *Alice in the Looking Glass* fashion. And there he is—the great Western strong-man-open-spaces type and a life of relentless action! But after all, what am I going to do about it? After all, there he is and I've got to go. . . . Don't wish me happiness—I don't expect to be happy, but it's gotten beyond that, somehow. Wish me courage and strength and a sense of humor—I will need them all.

---

[*] Pages 248-249 (Harcourt Brace Jovanovich, Inc., 1971, 1972).

There he is and I've got to go. It was as good an explanation as any.

I felt the plane lose altitude. The cabin was getting a bit stuffy, and seat belts snapped and unsnapped as people adjusted themselves and their belongings for the arrival in Lubumbashi. I leaned over to tuck the book away again, but first took another look at the last two sentences.

Well, I'm not marrying Charles Lindbergh, I thought. I'll need the courage and strength and the sense of humor, but I do expect to be happy. And I *will* be happy.

3
The Last Place in the World . . .

The plane circled lower. As it tipped my side of the aisle downward, I saw beneath me dry brown grass and, suddenly, a network of meandering footpaths through that grass, like snail tracks on the seashore. But wasn't I landing in the second largest city in the whole country? The plane turned, and all I could see was hazy blue, again.

So below me was Africa. It was the last place in the world I had ever wanted to live. Somehow, slipped in along with love and the spirit of adventure, I had a whole new culture to deal with. Humid jungles and bright sun held no charms for me with my bias toward autumn leaves and apple cider. Even as a child, my feelings were negative as missionaries flashed up one slide after another. Rows of unreal African faces dark against white-painted buildings. A ghostly faced American totally out of place at the end of the row, but trying to look as if he belonged. Could one belong? I wasn't counting on it. So what was this Africa below me? It was the place where Robby was, that's all I knew.

The plane tipped again to a distant view of tall smokestacks at the copper refinery, then righted itself for the final sweep low to the runway.

Now I could see people on the paths I had seen from farther up; men paused to stare upward at the huge jet thundering toward them; a mother clutched a crying baby tighter in the cloth that wrapped around the two of them; a girl reached up to support the pan of greens on her head in the blast of wind that would whip her at our passing.

And then we were down. I busied myself with reassuring little rituals of unfastening the seat belt and hoisting the heavy flight bag to my shoulder. He would be here. He had to be. After two years and eight thousand miles, the next step had to be his. I had exhausted both my one-way ticket and my courage.

The late-morning sun struck my face as I stepped out onto the stairs. I was dazzled, looking across the expanse of concrete. There were barbed wire barriers and the vivid orange flower of the tall, broad-leaved trees that flanked the airport. Then I saw Robby's slight, straight figure heading out toward the plane, looking like a lone car going the wrong way down a one-way street, against the stream of disembarking passengers.

Wedged in the slow-moving crowd, bumped by bags and elbows, I had no free hand to wave a wild greeting on my way down the stairs. It didn't matter. Our eyes met over the crowd. As soon as he was sure I was there, Robby turned to stroll slowly back toward the terminal, briefcase in hand exactly like the scores of passengers now crowding toward the terminal with their hand luggage.

What kind of a reception was this! There was just a split second to feel the shock of rejection before I understood. Of course, no one was allowed through that barbed wire; reunions with international passengers were not to happen on the tarmac; but somehow Robby was there, mingling with the passengers, walking slower and slower, so that he might pass with me through the rigorous testing points of immigration and customs.

My feet were quicker, and before we were stopped in the queue, I had nonchalantly edged up beside him. He reached for my attaché case, and we stood there, passports and health cards in hand. To the crowd around us, we were just another travel-worn couple bracing themselves for an hour or two of airport hassling.

I kept stealing glances, though. Yes, his eyes were blue as ever; the tropical sun had bronzed his arms and face; his hair was shorter than I had known it in Virginia; but skinny! So that's why I had brought the fruitcake and cookbook that even now were straining the muscles of the hand clutching the flight bag. Suddenly they were worth every outrageous dollar I had paid back at Patrick Henry Airport.

Robby handed both our passports to the immigration officials, who studied them several long moments—too long to suit me—and finally stamped us both as new arrivals in the Congo. To this day, technically Robby should still be there, his stamped arrivals in the country outnumbering his departures by one!

The last door was before us, and on the other side, we would be Robby meeting Susan, not the Ackermans arriving in Lubumbashi on a flight originating in Brussels. But as the door swung open to us and the baggage, there were shouts from the other side.

"Hey, Robby! I don't believe it! You really did get her here! Congratulations!" People were shaking my

27

hand and talking right past me. I felt like a remarkable piece of air freight that had successfully passed customs.

"What's that big smile doing on your face?" somebody was teasing Robby. What smile? I hadn't seen one yet. But when I took a sideways glance, there it was, a grin of pure delight, a we-really-did-it sort of grin, for all his friends.

Several young Congolese men appeared to shake my hand and express their amazement that this young American, whose motorcycle was well-known about town, was actually investing in a wife, mail-order, no doubt.

Someone called out, "We'll meet you for lunch over at the Mine Mess!" Someone else mentioned car keys and something that needed to be picked up at the post office before noon.

Mine Mess? That didn't exactly sound like Nick's Seafood Pavilion. I followed the crowd to the parking lot. So many people I didn't know were talking and filling up the space between and around Robby and me that I wondered if I was really there. Did he know everyone in this town? Would I ever be able to sort any of these people out, their names, what language they spoke, what relationship we were supposed to have? Numbly, I got into the front seat of the little Volkswagen and allowed myself to be driven toward the French-fries-and-meat-for-under-a-dollar of the mining company's mess hall.

An hour or two later, Robby was unlocking the door to a small white cottage hidden under vines that spilled tiny gold trumpets like rain.

"I'm house-sitting," he explained as a huge black Belgian sheepdog ran toward him, wagging his tail. "Hi, Bismarck, old boy. Bob and Lieve have left on vacation and want us to stay here till they get back next month."

"It's awfully pretty. Look at all the copper on the walls." I admired the beaten copper plaques depicting African life; the early afternoon sun struck the largest one of dancers gyrating around a drum, and it glowed red-gold like live coals in the quiet living room. "There must be lots of copper work here, because of all the mining," I said. "Is there?"

Robby didn't answer. He had set the bags inside, turned the key in the lock, and turned to me. Again I understood. Small talk time was over; friends and well-wishers were forgotten; now was the time for the airport greeting—only a few hours delayed and none the worse for it.

The sun's glow had left the copper dim and cold, in fact had disappeared altogether, when Robby remembered that we were invited to the Enright's for the evening.

"I know you'll like them," he said. "Ken and Lorraine have been like father and mother to me here. And they've offered to have you stay with them till the wedding. In fact, they *insisted* that you stay there. I think they were afraid I had ideas of my own."

"Tell me more about them," I said.

"He's a Methodist missionary, preacher, pilot, magician, storyteller. He's lived in the Congo for at least twenty years, and always on the edge of adventure. And, incidentally," he gave me a squeeze, "without his intervention you probably wouldn't even be here."

So it was Ken Enright who had made possible this maverick year ahead of us. Anyone who knows Mennonite Central Committee's Pax program knows too that Paxmen didn't get married. It just *wasn't done.* A Paxman was a single volunteer existing on $22 a

29

month over room and board as he served in an agricultural, educational, or other capacity in a developing country.

This was July, and Robby's 27-month term with Pax was to come to an end in September of that year. For the entire two years, his services had been on loan to the United Methodist Church in Lubumbashi. Though he helped in many different ways, his main job had been the accounting for the Centre Sociale Methodiste, which was a conglomerate of classes and recreational programs for many who were not accepted in regular secondary schools. Classes included typing, shorthand, cooking, sewing, and child care. A small library was maintained. Robby ended up teaching as well. By the time I arrived, he had climbed or rather tumbled by default into the position of director of the whole program. That was why the church there was interested in having Robby stay for another year after his two-year term as a Paxman had expired.

"But I can't," he had explained. "I've been waiting these two years to go back and get married. I don't feel like making it three."

"That's no problem," said Ken. "I'll send her a ticket. You can get married out here." It appeared that nothing was ever a problem to Ken Enright for very long.

Robby was the same way. The question of whether a Paxman could marry during his term of service seemed unimportant in light of the encouragement MCC usually gave to those who wished to extend their term of service. (Or was it unimportant in light of Robby's determination to marry me this particular year?) Just to be on the safe side, however, Robby decided not to mention that he was married until after the fact. In case somehow plans didn't work out, one wouldn't want MCC-Congo Director Vern Preheim upset all for nothing.

It was dusk, a sudden, heavy African dusk that turned abruptly into night as we stepped out onto the street to walk the few blocks to the Enrights' house. The air was thick with the smell of unfamiliar flowers, and something else sweet and heavy as incense.

As we turned up Avenue Likasi, I had to turn out on the street to avoid a hodgepodge of cardboard boxes and bamboo and a sheet or two of tin. In the shelter of this "house of cards" several dark figures crouched around a glowing fire.

"It's what they're burning that smells," I said.

"Charcoal," Robby explained. "They make it in the forests here."

"Those people don't live there, do they?" I whispered into Robby's ear as we picked our way back to the broken sidewalk.

"In a way," he answered. "Those men are guards. They're hired to sit all night guarding someone's business or home."

It seemed strange, but I supposed I would get used to it. The spikes and broken glass set into concrete walls, though, I would never get used to. As Robby clanged on a nine-foot-high iron gate that was chained with a padlock into such a concrete wall, I almost shuddered.

So this was a missionary, I thought. I had imagined something a little closer to the idea of "let me live in a house by the side of the road and be a friend to man." A guard trotted from somewhere behind the house, and the big gates swung open for us.

Inside the lighted living room, a warm and vivacious Lorraine Enright gave me a welcoming hug.

"We've heard so much about you, Susan, and we're so glad you're finally here. Robb has really been counting the days." I felt instantly at home in the laughter and banter that ensued. Ken's wild laugh broke out every few minutes. Robby and Eileen, the eleven-year-old, picked up the weapons of some ancient and unsettled battle, and ice cubes were disappearing down backs before I could figure out what they were fighting about. I could smell roast beef and saw that the table was set with china and a lace tablecloth. It was a Sunday dinner-type celebration. I followed Lorraine to the kitchen.

For the moment, I had forgotten I was in Africa. But a white-aproned man looked up from the popovers he was taking from the oven. "Jambo, mama," he said. A little uncertainly, I replied, "Jambo," hoping that was the correct Swahili response. Lorraine gave me the napkins to put around, but it was only a token task. The experts were in control.

Considering my cooking experience, I was a bit relieved not to be put to the test, but at the same time I felt a bit cheated, too. I had been all ready to assume my wifely burden. On the other hand, maybe after all I'd just always be Susan, the one that slipped out to shoot basketball with the boys while older cousins wiped dishes after family reunions.

At dinner Ken started in. "Saw your *projets de mariage* up on the courthouse bulletin board. You sure you followed all the regulations? Suppose they say you can't be married next week, that Susan should have been here a whole month, or something?"

"The *projets de mariage* have been tacked up there for all Lubumbashi to see for the past month," Robby assured everyone. "Of course, they don't know she's just arriving, but that shouldn't matter."

"And nobody's made any objection to the idea, eh?" Ken teased. "None of these young French or Congolese girls about town will show up at the last minute to put a stop to it?"

"Can't think of any that would," Robby said. "But you never know."

There seemed to be no other topic in the missionary community than the approaching wedding. Knowing nobody, I had pictured a quiet trip to the courthouse and then an equally quiet one to the altar for a few sacred words. Just two months before, I had enjoyed the maid of honor's place at my sister Sharon's wedding, soft yellow dresses, the teasing of the uncles, the lovely tiered cake richly decorated with lilies-of-the-valley, the going-away car all rattly with tin cans and old shoes. It was a time of family closeness and celebration, and it satisfied my need for the same. Now, as far as I was concerned, having boarded that airplane in Newport News amid sprinkles of rice and flowers was as much as to say the marriage was already done.

But I hadn't counted on the need for diversion in the missionary community as well as their kindness in wanting to help create memories for the two of us. Lorraine took me into the bedroom to show me the frilly blue dress her four-year-old Elinda could wear as the flower girl. And there was a paper plate, cleverly disguised with lace and cloth, to be curled into a flower basket from which to scatter franzy-pansy petals. I was impressed, but, not knowing what "franzy-pansies" were, I pictured some wildly fringed pansy faces, not my first choice for a wedding. I was to learn later that she was referring to the perfectly molded and perfumed white-pink-yellow frangipani blossoms of the tropics. There could have been none better!

Mary Ruth Reitz and Pat Rothrock showed up to report that they had traced the ancient candelabra that had been forged out of local iron for some wedding decades past. "But you'll have to look for tapers," they told me. "There may be some in town. You never know here."

Lorraine went on with the plans: "The Welchals are making mints for the reception. And all the Swiss teachers will be bringing salads."

"Swiss teachers?" I heard myself say a bit uncertainly. "Oh."

"And they've offered to sing, too. But you'll have to choose some songs. Of course, Mrs. Kendall will play the wedding march on the organ."

"Don't forget to look around town for canned hams. The wholesale grocers may have something. And the cake. I suppose we could come up with something in the way of pans."

"We'll just find a bakery in town," Robby said firmly, as if things were getting too involved to suit him. "I'm sure there are some Congolese who know how to bake cakes. And, by the way, we've changed the location of the reception. It'll be at the Kendalls instead of the Welchals."

"That's fine with me," I said, not having met either family as yet. Kendalls? Welchals? I sighed. It didn't feel like this could possibly be *my* wedding we were discussing. Weddings were once-in-a-lifetime events! Planning one's wedding was a favorite Sunday afternoon game for teenage girls. We tried to dream up exotic color combinations, special flowers, and unconventional sites such as on the top of a cliff above the pounding sea or in a Williamsburg rose garden. The groom was always a shadowy and unimportant figure in the event, lost in the grandeur of *the wedding it-*

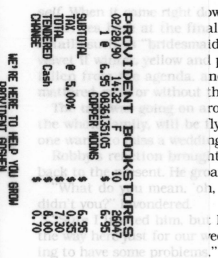

...own to it, I had reversed my ...al moment. All-consuming ...ds in burgundy and cream ...pink voile if summer" had ...nd it was only Robby that ...the trapping of a wedding. ...round me. "And Amstutzes, ...lying in from Kapanga! No ...ng." Lorraine was beaming. ...it my wandering thoughts ...aned. "Oh, no!"

...n, no'? You did invite him,

: I didn't think he'd fly all ...edding. I'm afraid we're go-...."

...ould a missionary pilot, fa-ther of four, cause? I was to have that question answered fully in just a few more days.

4
Hostage for Christian Marriage

If Robby had made himself a list of things to do the morning of July 10, it would have run something like this:

7:30 Rendezvous with plumber
9:00 Get married
10:00 Buy candles for Saturday wedding
11:00 Pay teachers' salaries
12:00 Lunch

On my list, there was only the one: Get married.

The Enrights' kitten had awakened me with a rough face-washing, in the little bedroom I was sharing with one of the girls. It was early enough that no one was stirring in the house, but after a week of slipping in late and getting up early, I had mastered the padlock system on the several doors I had to exit through. The big iron gate with the spikes was luckily already unlocked.

The sun was just high enough to flood the crowded street, filled with workers streaming to the copper refinery on foot, on bicycles, and now and then a packed, lumbering bus spewing billows of black exhaust fumes. I passed a mother sitting at the edge of the street with several small children clustered around her sharing a long stick of bread with a soft, ripe avocado as spread. The beggars were already out, too, some swinging by on one crutch, others with shriveled legs deposited at busy street corners by a relative. Ahead of me walked, like princesses, several young women in rich wax print wrap-skirts, blouses bright as hibiscus blossoms, and an intricately wound head cloth. How did they manage to look so beautiful on such low family income? They were gorgeous, and I looked down at my plain khaki skirt and simple sandals with something like surprise at how drab and pale an aspect I presented.

I turned in under the blue-sprinkled jacaranda tree, where the sign said *Mbwa Mkali*. Bismarck didn't look nearly as fierce as the sign was meant to convey, but seemed thrilled to have me open the gate and walk in.

What with the plumber on his mind, and the rest of the details of the day still to be arranged, Robby seemed a bit distant. "Everything's got to go smoothly," he said, "to get everything done. I hope the plumber's on time."

The plumber *was* on time, and just before nine o'clock, the two of us ventured down a long, dark, gritty hall in Commune Lubumbashi, the administrative center for our district of the city. Robby knew the secretary well by this time; he had been in his office three or four times that week, making sure of the appointment time.

The man looked startled, glanced down at his dossier of papers, and asked, "You're here for the marriage?"

"Yes," Robby replied. "Remember we changed the

hour from eleven to nine."

"Of course," the secretary replied. "The marriage hall is this way."

He showed us a clean and sunny room, where windows let in the brisk air of midwinter July. A platform was raised at one end, and on it a heavy wooden table presided in front of a carved love seat. The secretary pointed to the love seat and then made a quick exit. I looked at Robby; Robby looked at me. The room seemed terribly empty as we sat down side by side. I spread the lace-trimmed skirts of my demure navy blue dress and felt the high lace of its collar. There was a silence.

Ken Enright walked in then, joking with Len Clarke, a tall black American who was currently vice-consul in Lubumbashi. Mr. Clarke had to witness the marriage to make it legal in the U.S. Slipping in behind them was Morgan Kenani, the young teacher whom Robby had asked to sign our marriage certificate, co-witness along with Ken Enright. Morgan, whose self-effacement was his one irritating characteristic, slipped into a chair in the back of the room, barely noticed, while Ken and Mr. Clarke, still talking and laughing, found the two extra chairs beside the love seat.

From time to time a splendidly dressed Congolese woman opened the door, looked in, and left again, agitated and distressed. Finally she entered the room to explain in careful French that the secretary did not have all the papers in order as yet.

Another fifteen minutes ticked by. Man-type small talk washed over me as I felt suspended in time and space. Maybe this morning was after all just a dream, and this period of nothing happening would stretch on and on until I awoke, smiling to myself. I imagined myself telling my family, over coffee, that I had dreamed I was in Africa about to be married to Robby, but that the people couldn't locate the proper papers. My sandal gritted against some tiny grains of sand on the floor as I shifted my position, and the possibility of it being a dream seemed pretty remote, after all. I slipped my hand across Robby's knee and into his hand. Yes, there was the little brown mole inside the third finger of his right hand.

Madame Mayoress glided in, the distressed look gone from her smooth brown face and in its place one of utmost solemnity under the ornate turban. We stood as she took her place behind the table. A heavy, thick book lay open before her, but before turning to it, she picked up a weighty satin sash of blue, red, and yellow. Wrapping it symbolically around her waist, she became the Democratic Republic of the Congo personified, with all the dignity adhering thereto expressed in her slim, regal figure.

When she began to read the handwritten page before her, I could sympathize with the secretary and the forty-minute delay. I was hearing, in French, all the details of our births and existences heretofore. I don't think Nina Viola Stemen Yoder, mother of the bride, would have recognized her name as it fell from the lips of this beautiful woman, nor would Dorothy Dean Heinlein Baxter, mother of the groom, but it all went to show how little understanding had to do with things.

Suddenly there was a silence directed at me. The rhythm of the French phrases had been broken, and what was I to say? Certainly not "I do." *"Oui!"* I squeaked out. It was only later that I read the fine print to see that I had promised to obey the commands of this man by my side. That wasn't really news to me, after all. When his voice had come crackling over that ham radio set in Virginia saying "I want you to come and marry me," I had said "When?" hadn't I?

After we had signed our names in the huge book, the witnesses stepped up to do the same. Madame Mayoress turned to Mr. Clarke: "Monsieur Morgan Kenani?"

Finding that he was Mr. Clarke, a name not found on her document, she sent him packing to the back of the room and summoned the apologetic Morgan forward to make his elaborate signature, though it nearly paralyzed the young teacher to know he had preference over an American consul.

"Félicitations!" The woman who had married us removed her satin sash and warmly congratulated us. "And here are your official documents," she went on, handing us a giant sheet of paper and some booklets. All our vital statistics had been painstakingly but not very accurately typed onto the giant sheet of paper—again I thought of the poor hassled secretary.

Robby opened one of the smaller gray pasteboard booklets and looked up at me with mischief in his eye: "I thought you were just trying to scare me off when you said you wanted a dozen children!"

Eyebrows raised. I looked inside my booklet. There were neat blocks devoted to the future entry of each of the names of—not twelve, but up to twenty-four children! I was ready to frame a teasing reply, when I noticed that beside the date of birth was a block for the date of death.

And our laughter faded, because gray as the cardboard book cover was the Congolese reality of fifty percent infant mortality. It wasn't a wedding-day thought, but then neither were the troops of beggars that flocked around as we got out of the car at the shop most likely to sell decorative candles in Lubumbashi.

And luck was with us. Indeed they did have a dozen long white tapers in stock. Robby seemed pleased that the list of things to do that day was ticking itself off so nicely, when a very British voice broke in.

"Why, Robby Ackerman, good to see you, man! How are you?"

A tall, white-haired but youngish-looking man was shaking Robby's hand and then mine.

"Susan, this is Horace Butler. Horace, I'd like you to meet my friend Susan Yoder," Robby said proudly. "She's just come out from the States."

"How smashing!" said Horace enthusiastically. "I hope she's getting around to see the sights. You really ought to take her up to see the falls at Lubudi. They're so wild and beautiful—all those exquisite little yellow begonias blooming in the rocks around the falls."

Whatever Robby was replying was totally lost on me. Susan Yoder, my foot. Hadn't we just a few minutes ago promised to be man and wife? Weren't we married? But that must have been another foolish dream of mine. I know it didn't *seem* real, this strange way of marrying, and maybe it really wasn't. Maybe, like a bad batch of smallpox vaccine, the ceremony didn't "take." My indignation rose. Just come out from the States to see him, huh? Well, I had news for him. This was supposed to be the beginning of forever, and if he couldn't accept the idea of being married and having a wife sooner or later, this wasn't going to be much fun for either one of us.

". . . Victoria Falls on our honeymoon," I picked up suddenly on the conversation that had gone on without me. "So I think maybe we'll make it to the Lubudi Falls later in the year." Robby put his arm around my shoulders. "Ken Enright's marrying us on Saturday at the little chapel at the theological school at Mulungwishi."

It all comes, I thought sheepishly, of getting married two days before your wedding day. We couldn't really call ourselves married, but just for a moment there, fingering those gray booklets with space for twenty-four children. . . .

Perhaps Robby's nonchalant attitude wasn't all that sincere, either. Anyway, that evening at the Enright's, he stood and stretched soon after nine o'clock. "Well, I guess I'll take Susan on home with me. We're married now, you know." Seeing Ken's quick look of protest, he went on: "You signed the papers yourself this morning, Ken. You can't deny that we're married!"

"Oh, no, you don't!" Ken sputtered. "You two are going to be married on Saturday morning and not a moment before! I've got a sermon all made out on Christian marriage, and I don't want you two to be like many of our pastors who get around to the religious ceremony ten kids and ten years too late. Everybody's watching you two here, and you've got to be an example. Susan's staying right here with us tonight!"

Robby just grinned at me, the hostage for Christian marriage, and shrugged as if to concede that he really couldn't have expected a much different response from a Methodist minister.

5
The Ticking Ferns

Robby's hands jerked the steering wheel to miss another pothole in the road. Just because we were on the one stretch of paved road in the whole province of Katanga didn't mean we were exempt from potholes; it just made the jolts harder when they came. I craned my neck back over the seat to see if the big square box of wedding cake was still right-side-up. The bouquet of pink roses from some kind Belgian lady I hadn't even met had pitched forward on its head, but somehow it didn't matter. This time tomorrow, our second and final wedding ceremony would be over and the roses would be fading, anyhow.

This was my first ride out of the city, out of the circuit of missionary houses, into Africa. The Peugeot station wagon itself, purring along and smelling of civilization's gasoline fumes and plastic, seemed out of its place and time, not to mention the candelabra leaning rakishly over the white-frosted and silver-spangled wedding cake.

The terrain of this inland plateau was savanna-land, or "high bush." There were jagged spears of coarse high grass, the occasional scrubby tree or patch of forest, and, for variety, the peaks of red-clay termite mounds as much as thirty feet high. I saw children climbing around one of the mounds, bend-

43

ing to scratch and dig as if looking for buried treasure.

"What could be growing on a termite mound?" I asked. "It looks like those children are gathering something to eat, like roots, or. . . ."

"Or termites," Robby answered.

Though I could plainly see that it was so, the concept was not one that my Western mind could absorb quickly. "They're eating termites? They must be starving, to do that!"

"Not at all. It's termite season, and termites are a delicacy. You'll see tubs of them at the market. Fried up crisp, a good source of oil and minerals and protein in the diet. Some of them are an inch long, and nice and plump."

"It sounds like you've had firsthand experience," I said suspiciously.

"I have," he said. "They're kind of chewy, like bacon rinds. But you do have to be careful to pull the heads off before you pop them in your mouth. A friend of mine had a sore throat for days when a termite bit him back, going down his throat."

I turned back to the window, deliberately ignoring the termite hills this time as I scanned the tropical scenery. Here and there were clusters of green bushes made up of dozens of half-closed parasols of leaves, interspersed with stalks of some weed that looked a lot like corn. If it weren't so random and sparse, one would have thought it had been planted by human beings.

"Not quite like Iowa, is it?" Robby broke into my thoughts.

"You mean that really is corn? These are corn fields?" I looked again at the foreign pattern of the rows—or the absence of rows.

"They grow good corn around here. And between the corn plants, that's manioc, or cassava there, the green bushes. People eat the root like a potato or dried and pounded into flour, and the leaves cooked as greens. The cultivating and planting is all done with a hoe less than eighteen inches long—that and wife power. Wives are quite an asset here, and that's why four or five aren't uncommon, if a man can afford it. People have been asking how many goats and cows I had to pay for you. I tell them you were a bargain to begin with, but that I'll have to keep paying for you the rest of my life."

"Sorry I didn't bring my hoe along, but then I think my bags were heavy enough as it was!" We laughed and then rode along in silence, as the sun sank toward the west. The two-hour drive from Lubumbashi to Mulungwishi was nearly over, and the road had changed to sand and gravel. As we slowed to pass through treacherous sand beds, I saw the patient, closed expression on the face of a woman waiting in the tall grass for our vehicle to pass, balancing a huge pan of cassava roots on her head and adjusting the cloth of a big-eyed baby who was looking over her shoulder at the noisy car.

Robby drove on, in preoccupied silence. Finally, I asked, "Are you nervous?"

"Well, I'm not at all relaxed," he answered. "Are you?"

"I'm a little dazed," I answered. "Everything's so strange, it's almost as if it's not happening to me at all, as if nothing I say or do makes any difference. I guess I'm sort of waiting for the wedding part to be over with so we can get on with our lives."

Robby agreed. "It's not marriage I'm apprehensive about, and certainly not *you* I'm afraid of. It's the wedding." He paused. "No, it's not the wedding so much as the car."

"The car?" It seemed to be running along the bumps and dips like any car should.

"You see, Harold Amstutz, the pilot from Kapanga, and John Pannabecker are just going to destroy this car. I know it. And I don't want to drive you back to Lubumbashi in a soaped-up, shaving-creamed, toilet paper and tin can affair with several spark plugs missing. I've been trying to figure out a way to make them drive this car back to Lubumbashi after the ceremony instead of me. That's what's making me nervous."

If it was only once in a lifetime, I didn't see anything wrong with shaving cream and a few tin cans. It seemed to go along naturally with white veils and wedding cake. But I could see that with Robby it was a matter of principle, something that only another practical joker could understand.

I left Robby to wrestle with this major problem and looked out at the evening scenery once more. Much of the landscape was charred black by the fires set by farmers to make the job of cultivation easier, when the rains would come a few months later. We passed a small village. In the dim glow of a low pot of coals, I could see the closely gathered family, and behind them, the black opening of the thatched-roof hut. What was life like around that fire? Inside that door? I might just as well be looking through the pages of the *National Geographic*, for all the insight I had as I sailed past in the white Peugeot.

And then we were climbing, past a large church, past a small chapel, past a number of school buildings. This was Mulungwishi. Roland and Monica Baumann were expecting us for dinner and would be my hosts for the night, while Robby was to stay with Stefan Fischer and his snakes and monkeys at the top of the hill.

The pleasing monotone of cowbells enchanted me, as Monica showed me upstairs to the cozy study-turned-guest-room for the night. Fresh pink flowers hung out of a niche in the wall, and two bright-green parrots shared my room from their window cage. An earthenware plate beside my bed held an orange and a banana as well as a tiny bar of Swiss chocolate; an English New Testament and prayer book were next to the fruit. These people didn't know me, and here I was, treated like visiting royalty, or—like a bride! Maybe the myth attached to being a bride had some reality after all. Anyway, I could feel the celebration surrounding me like confetti at a parade. In the quiet little room, it was a shield from the lonely, empty feeling that threatened as my mind wandered to my sisters' weddings, and the hectic excitement that always prevailed the night before.

I remembered Linda getting up in the middle of the night and tiptoeing down to the kitchen to make sure the wedding cake on which Mother had spent all afternoon was properly protected from ants, roaches, and water bugs, the scourges of the humid Tidewater summers. I remembered driving the four hours from Harrisonburg to Newport News the night before Sharon's wedding and coming in with my arms full of bridesmaid's dresses without hems or buttonholes. I could hear Sharon saying, "Didn't I say she wouldn't have them finished?" and myself answering, "Don't worry, there's plenty of time!" and then working late into the night. I guess we did end up pinning a cuff or two, where it didn't show.

I remembered watching Linda pack her honeymoon

suitcase. Growing thoughtful, she suddenly said, "Can I give you your present now for being my maid of honor?" I got a present, did I? At fifteen, I was thrilled enough with the pink organdy dress with a cummerbund and my first white high-heeled shoes. I opened her gift, a flowered, zippered travel case for toilet articles, and was admiring it when she said, in true Linda fashion, "Now can I borrow it for the honeymoon?"

This night, July 11, wasn't going to be that kind of night, I could tell. It was going to be just me and the parrots.

A door opened and closed downstairs and I heard voices. Was that Robby's? I left the parrots blinking and flew down the stairs. It was Robby, on his way back from an inspection tour of the little chapel.

"The tapers are in the candelabra," he said, "and the ferns off Al Welchal's front porch are safely in each corner."

"I thought you were already up the hill with the snakes and monkeys," I said. "The thought of it made me glad I have parrots instead!"

"I'm not very sleepy yet," he said. "Want to take a little walk with me to the top of the hill?"

My arm slipped around his back and his around mine as we walked to the top of the "Swiss Hill." The sky was so wide and starry that the path was plain. A monkey trilled a sleepy warning chatter from Stefan's huge enclosure as we passed his, the last house. Robby guided me to a big rock, and as I sat, I resolutely cast from my mind the possibility that any of the friends and relations of Stefan's snakes were camping out in the vicinity.

There was silence around and between us. I felt something like a bride in an arranged marriage must feel—not terribly well-acquainted with the man I was about to promise my life to. Well, it had been two years since we'd really been together. You could hardly count these last few days.

Let's see; I could say, "Well, this is it!" No, too flippant. How about, "Guess what happens tomorrow!" No, that was childish. Why didn't *he* say something?

In the black distance a steady light appeared. The light grew larger and with it, down the track below us, a steam engine came panting, tooting its whistle mournfully and then trailing off into the blackness to the west, its rhythm echoing into the night for a long time.

"What's tomorrow really going to bring for us?" Robby spoke suddenly.

Was there an answer to that? If so, I didn't know it.

He went on. "I feel like one little star in that whole huge sky, and I wonder what I'm supposed to be doing up there."

So he had that lonely feeling too. I snuggled closer, suddenly feeling warmed and needed. "I know," I whispered. "But now we'll be two stars. Maybe that'll be friendlier. And brighter."

What with cackling chickens and goats with bells and parrots who knew how to whistle, my wedding morning started rather early. My first feeling was one of relief. The day had finally come and would just as surely go. All the good-byes I'd already said, the long journey, the civil ceremony—all seemed like just so many false starts. From now on, there would be no more being passed around from one spare bed to another. I would be with Robby, wherever that might be.

Monica had baked a crusty whole grain loaf in her outdoor clay oven, and we lingered over our bread and coffee. I stroked the velvet petals of the dainty orange flower by my plate as she read an English prayer for me in her homey Swiss accent. I already felt blessed. How could the day—and the future—be otherwise?

It was quiet in the little upstairs room as I stepped into the cream-colored dress and struggled with the long back zipper. I needed a bridesmaid, I thought ruefully. I had always assumed it would be Bunni, with as many of my sisters as was practical besides. Who was supposed to slip on this blue garter? I wondered, opening the little box that Aunt Frances Smucker had given me at the trousseau shower. Aunt Frances's birthday was today, July 12, so she had taken a special interest from afar in the festivities. There was a lucky sixpence, shiny and new, to tuck into the toe of my shoe, and there was the lacy blue garter. I pulled the garter up over my knee. Well, anyway, I was sure of having help getting it off.

From a pocket of my suitcase I took one last thing. It was a tiny butterfly pin of Belgian lace. "Wear this for me," Nancy had said the week before as we came out of the lace-maker's shop in Brussels' Grand' Place. The creamy butterfly touched my shoulder lightly as if to bless me with its fragile happiness. I thought of Nancy, who had come as far with me as she could. Why, I had had my maid of honor, I thought. And as for the "something borrowed" that every bride needs—I would borrow her courage.

Just before eleven, I walked down the hill with Monica and into a dusty library beside the chapel. Monica pinned the simple circular veil onto my long, smoothly brushed hair and, giving me a well-wishing pat, hurried off to join the others who were going to sing.

The door opened and Robby slipped in, looking strained and pale.

"Harold Amstutz got here," he muttered. "I know he's up to something, too. He was running around the chapel with a huge grin on his face earlier this morning."

"So?" I felt gay and giddy. "We should all be wearing big grins. Where's yours? In a few minutes we'll be married, and who cares about Harold Amstutz, whoever he is?"

Obviously, Robby did.

Then I heard music. Mrs. Kendall had begun to play the little pump organ, and a cold flip-flop in the pit of my stomach told me that this time it was for me. Elinda Enright was dancing around, trying at the same time to keep the frangipani petals in her little basket, and I told her to go ahead and start up the aisle, tossing them out. We crossed over the red dirt to the chapel door. As I reached up to feel if my veil had started to slide off, I met the solemn gaze of a dozen uninvited Africans hanging around outside the door. For a fleeting moment I felt utterly ridiculous in the veil and ivory dress, like a relic from another planet or century.

The organ music came to an end, and then the Swiss Methodist voices harmonized in the opening words of "O Perfect Love," just like any Mennonite sextet back in Virginia, and we started in, my hand on Robby's arm. The beauty of the chapel took me by surprise. Huge potted ferns crowded the altar, and curled white lilies like cornucopias stood gracefully among them. In the dimness, the tapers were burning with that soft, intense light that is both festive and holy. The rough-hewn stone walls glowed in the rainbow light coming through the tiny square windowpanes of colored glass, and the few short benches were filled with the hushed presence of the thirty guests.

It was only a dozen steps or so until we were standing before Ken Enright and the golden, polished tree which held out its arms in the natural lines of a cross. Ken launched into an opening prayer, and as we bowed our heads, I noticed something. It was a noisy, ticking something, and it seemed to be located in the ferns to my left.

Nothing ticks as insistently as an old-fashioned wind-up alarm clock, and there's nothing alarm clocks do so well as to make noise when no one wants to hear it, like very early in the morning, or like in the middle of one's wedding ceremony. I felt Robby's sideways glance, and I knew he was hearing it too. Even Ken, as he came up from his prayer, cast a moment's wary look at that thick ferny mass that seemed to have grown a metallic heart. For a moment I thought that Ken might pause in the sermon he was beginning and take a minute to rummage in the ferns himself.

I was going to giggle. I knew that feeling all too well. Not at your wedding, Susan. I tried to get a firm grip on myself. But the clock clacked on. Would it ring? When would it ring? I began to picture the horrid specimen of humanity this Harold Amstutz must be. And still I felt that giggle bubbling up. Maybe I could turn it into a radiant bridal smile. Looking up at Ken, I burst into a smile that must have stretched from one side of my veil to the other.

He was just getting wound up and didn't notice me. Today was his long-awaited chance to preach about Christian marriage to the African pastors who were among the invited guests.

"How many years has this chapel been standing here, and today we see the first young couple that has ever stood before this altar to be joined together by God as man and wife! The first couple!" The sermon went on and on, and so did the ticking of the clock. Perhaps if the clock hadn't been distracting me, I could have figured out what was "Christian" about this wedding of ours. Was it the flower girl's lace-covered paper plate basket? Was it the ticking ferns? There were prayers, of course, and a minister, but if prayers and sermons were a part of the normal life of the couple after and before the wedding, would a civil ceremony without them spell doom for the institution of Christian marriage? Or was a Christian marriage something that went beyond the ceremony, that. . . .

Clang! I braced myself for the horrendous blaring of the alarm, but with that one muted peal, the clock only ticked on as before. So the villain had a heart after all. Sneaking around the chapel with a grin on his face, to quote Robby, he had gone to push the button in before the alarm had the chance to blare its rude noise into the hush of the wedding chapel.

Ken faltered only a brief moment, then began to bring his message to a close. In a matter of minutes we were saying, "I will," and the marriage, for the second time that week, was over with. How thankful I was that Robby had earlier vetoed the idea of memorizing our vows and saying them to each other. With that clock ticking a bizarre obbligato, who knows what might have come out of our mouths?

And then we were out in the blinding noonday sun, everyone laughing and congratulating us. The car was already unrecognizable. Toilet paper streamed from the antenna. On the windshield was scrawled a desperate "Help!" We were pelted with a barrage of African rice, which found its way into every opening in our clothing as well as the car. We submitted to the short clattery ride up the "American Hill."

The Kendall residence was thrown open wide at every door and blossoming veranda. Women inside were rushing to set out the feast. Someone guided us to a post at the main door, to greet the incoming guests. At the recent weddings of my friends and sisters, I had taken my frilly apron and ladled punch, sliced cake, refilled nut bowls, or handed a pen to guests as they passed a guest register. Now all around me I saw people I barely knew whipping out the homemade colored fondant mints, laying out platters of the sliced ham we had scoured Lubumbashi to obtain, and arranging the gorgeous green-and-red salads over lacy tablecloths—and it was for me.

The hand-shaking began. Smiling was easy, and that seemed to be all that was required of me. Talk washed all around me, in Swahili, English, some Swiss, and a bit of French. One tall, dignified older man was introduced to me as Pastor Morrison, district superintendent of the Methodist churches of the area. I could hardly keep from staring at his feet. Shoeless, his feet seemed to have developed a kind of armor out of his own skin, which was cracked and furrowed like dried and overused leather. As he greeted me, I was conscious of my own creamy-white slippers smooth over nylons and was relieved that my dress was long enough to keep them from his view as we stood there together.

"Well, Robby! Congratulations! I never thought you'd really go through with this risky job! Of course, I was listening when you called and asked her to come out and marry you—real interesting conversation!"

"Well, it looked like—or sounded like—you've been doing your best to prevent it!" Robby answered as he shook hands with a stocky man in a gray suit and black tie. He was grinning hugely, the man was, and that's how I knew immediately who he was. A pretty wife with a head full of curls was tripping along beside him, and a golden-haired cherub in a blue party dress held his hand trustingly, obviously unaware that deep down he was a despicable villain. Looking at Elsie Amstutz's gay, friendly smile, somehow I knew that there had been no alarm clocks in the ferns at her wedding, nor had she known anything about the origins of the ticking she must surely have heard an hour ago!

"You're married, yes, but the day isn't over yet," Harold Amstutz warned. Did he ever stop grinning?

Somebody was calling us to cut the cake. The knife was beribboned and waiting. However, the cake was not quite the rich, golden pound cake my mother always baked for weddings. The big square concoction was lined with a tough pastry, full of hard silver spangles in a center of mocha cream—and was that a touch of rum or cognac? The cake part was a decidedly gray dusty color and tasted just like it looked, I was to discover. So much for Belgian-run Congolese bakery cakes, I thought, glad I wasn't the one who had to dispose of the leftovers.

We escaped the noisy living and dining room with our plates and found a bench outside under a red hibiscus bush. The food was delicious, but Robby wasn't paying much attention to it.

"Listen," he said in a low voice. "I think I've got something worked out."

"Oh?"

"When it's time to get into the car, act like you're

going to get in, but when I say so, run and jump into Al's green Peugeot and we'll head for the airstrip."

"We're going to fly back to Lubumbashi?"

"Ken said he'll take us in his plane. He must have taken pity on us after hearing the alarm clock."

We laughed, remembering the tense wedding ceremony that was already safely a part of the past. Then I remembered something else. "But you hate those little planes. You said you always get airsick, and I remember crossing the English Channel with you when you stayed seasick for three days."

"This is only a thirty-minute flight. I've got to get those guys back."

The remaining hours of eating and talking passed pleasantly, except for Robby's discovery that someone had removed his suitcase, his passport, and his briefcase from Stefan's house during the course of the celebration, but he dispatched the honest Stefan to recover them. The Swiss were a bit shocked at the wedding frivolity of the Americans by this time and were determined to help the bridal couple on their way.

At last it was time to go. Somehow the festive knot of well-wishers didn't seem like strangers to me any more. I hugged the sunny little flower girl and Lorraine Enright, "mother of the bride," and then we headed toward our car, which by now was trailing enough junk and decoration to double as a gypsy cart.

Then Robby shouted, "Now!"

We turned and swooped into the other car, which was parked innocently pointing its nose down the hill in the other direction. Ken piled in with us, and Al Welchal was already at the wheel. The blank surprise on every face was all I saw as the car lurched off and sped down the "American Hill" and off across the

Mulungwishi station in a direction that was new to me, disregarding ditches and potholes in its haste.

Robby's brow was still tense. "We've got to make sure Harold doesn't get out here in time to move his plane out onto the airstrip, because then Ken couldn't take off."

"But if they followed us right away, couldn't they get there by the time we get into the plane and easily have us blocked?" I objected.

Just then we bumped up onto the railroad crossing, over the track where the train had whistled so mournfully at midnight, and down the other side. I caught a glimpse of a large truck off to the right, and Robby, too, whirled around to get a closer look.

"Hey, perfect!" He laughed his loudest, happiest laugh—one that I hadn't heard for several days. "Look, Susan, look at the roadblock behind us now!"

Now I was sure that fate smiled on brides. "How in the world did that truck happen to pull out just then and stop crosswise in the road?" I was absolutely amazed. I was also extremely naive when it came to practical jokers and their ways.

"All it took was ten zaires," Robby said smugly. "And it's a ten-ton truck across that narrow lane. They'll never get around him."

"You paid that man to have the truck there?"

"Well, you wouldn't expect him to sit out there all Saturday afternoon for nothing, would you?"

We were already at the airstrip. Ken hurried through his safety checklist, while I squeezed into the five-seater Cessna 180 after Robby, somehow hanging onto my white bridal bouquet and the spray of red roses, too.

Ken was just swinging up into the pilot's seat when a Volkswagen came careening out across the grass in front of the plane.

"Let's go!" shouted Robby, but there was no possible way. The VW's doors exploded open, and Dick Kendall burst out, a big square box in his hand.

"Wait!" he yelled, and ran over to the plane.

We had no other choice. Now what? I thought. After the alarm clock, the car, the stolen suitcases, the ominous hints of Harold Amstutz—what could this be? A smoke bomb? A box of jumpy frogs? A snake?

"My wife thought you might like some of the leftover cake!" shouted Dick. He tossed the box, white and neatly tied with string, in through Ken's open door.

Waving and beaming at us, he got back into his car and drove off.

And then we were airborne, buzzing low over the crowd of people still clustered around Kendall's house and the car that had been decorated in vain, off and up into the smoky, hazy late afternoon sky. The plane seemed so fragile and tiny after the Boeing 707s I had just flown on. Responsive to every whip of wind, it bucked and danced its way southeast.

Late afternoon is Africa's worst time for flying, as the air heated by the sun for all those hours tends to get energetic, and air currents oppose each other vigorously. I felt just a bit like a cat in a car for the first time, wishing I could flatten myself under the seat and howl a little, too. I noticed the chalky shade of gray Robby's face had already assumed, and soon I was holding his head with one arm and keeping a sick sack at the ready with the other. How this could be better than driving a decorated car down the highway, I didn't know. We were submitting, I supposed, to principle alone.

Robby tried to fool his nausea by pretending to be asleep. But I had one burning question.

"How did Dick Kendall get that Volkswagen around the truck, with those impossible embankments on each side of the railroad track?"

Robby's eyelids never flickered. "It was Dick Kendall's truck," he whispered. "And his chauffeur. That's how."

6
Prisoners!

A good place to start a honeymoon is in a cozy, flower-covered cottage, especially when that cottage has a resident cook who knows what he's doing. Léonard used to cook for the Belgian governor of Katanga, and Bob and Lieve Vanhee, his present employers, prized him so much that they had had him fitted with a gorgeous set of false teeth when his own failed. I'm not sure that I ever saw Léonard's fine set of teeth, however, since Léonard didn't usually open his mouth. He was all action. Frankly, I was scared to death of him.

My worst fear was being surprised by him in the regions of the kitchen. I was glad I could hear him open the little back-porch door and had time to flee before he shuffled in barefooted, in a spotless white jacket. It wasn't because he was gruff-looking. It was because he was an expert, and I was just a bride with a new Betty Crocker cookbook and a history of skipping out of the kitchen whenever possible. Not only was I an inexperienced cook, but I was having culinary culture shock as well. Even the pots and pans in the Vanhees' cabinets were of different shapes and uses from the ones I knew, not to mention the lack of familiar ingredients.

But those concerns would surface later, after the

two-week honeymoon had been properly tended to, and we were back in Lubumbashi for the final month of house-sitting for the Vanhees. For the moment, I had only to savor that exquisite first breakfast as Mr. and Mrs. Robby Ackerman. There were crusty little rolls, bacon-tomato omelets, and European jam served on china and a starched white hemstitched tablecloth.

"Does Bismarck always bark so much?" I asked Robby after buttering my second roll. "He sounded absolutely beside himself during the night. I was beginning to think there was somebody prowling around. Did you hear him, too?"

Robby finished chewing his bread slowly and carefully, while I waited impatiently for the answer that looked like it wanted to come. I reminded myself that, to him, eating and talking were each all-consuming efforts and not to be undertaken within the same moment.

"I heard him, too. I got up and looked out the window several times in the night and didn't see anybody. But I don't think it was a thief. It might have been Harold and John just wanting to harass us. But I didn't worry. We're really locked up tight here, and I knew they couldn't bother us. I even went out and checked the car for sabotage, but it looks just fine where I parked it in the yard."

It was such a luxurious, leisurely morning that we just couldn't hurry to pack up the car for the wedding trip. In the early afternoon, though, Robby suddenly decided to get moving. We were going to head south over the Zambian border that night, and Robby explained that you wouldn't want to be caught at the border after dark.

"You have enough trouble during the day," he explained. "I never bribe the customs or immigration agents. But they think that it's always worth another try. One of these days this poor American will have some money, so they raise questions about the car papers, hem and haw over passports, go through everything in my suitcase twice, very slowly."

It didn't sound very appealing to me, and I anxiously looked at the sun. There was certainly a good four hours of sunshine before the rapid equatorial sunset, and the trip would take about three hours.

The car we were taking was a shiny white Dodge Dart, just huge by local standards. That car had quite a history. Eighteen months earlier, a Methodist church back in the States had donated it to the missionary work in the Congo. When it arrived in Lubumbashi, the poor car was in bad shape. All four thirteen-inch tires, rims, and brake drums had been stolen en route. There was no garage in all of Katanga equipped to provide the missing parts. So, for seventeen months, the "white elephant" sat on blocks. The eighteenth month—after realizing that his bride wasn't going to purchase four Dodge brake drums and carry them among her belongings to Africa—Robby got inventive. He and Alex, a Pakistani mechanic in Lubumbashi, took four brake drums from a junked Willys Jeep, cut the lug studs off and repositioned them so that they would fit a set of fifteen-inch Chevrolet tire rims, and installed the oversized fifteen-inch tires on the jeep brake drums. There were five lug studs on each wheel, and Alex could find only four lug nuts to go on them, but otherwise, the car was repaired and ready to go.

Alex had had the car waiting for the bridal couple getting shakily out of Ken's airplane the day before, and the sight of it had perked Robby up considerably.

The Dodge was roadworthy for the first time in eighteen months, and we had permission to let our honeymoon trip be her maiden voyage before she settled down to her intended work as missionary transportation.

All was ready for the first Ackerman family trip. I was taking my place in the front seat as Robby went to unlock the gates and swing them wide to allow the car to pass through.

What was taking him so long? And why was he just standing there looking up and down the street in that distracted way? Giving the closed gate a resentful rattle, he turned and came back to lean in my window.

"Now I understand Bismarck's barking," he said ruefully. "We're chained and padlocked inside this yard. I knew that was Harold and John out here last night."

So we were prisoners. I studied the fence which stretched around the small lot six feet high. Its concrete posts and metal poles were underscored by a riotous growth of thorny bougainvillea in gorgeous shades of rose and purple, as well as what everyone called that "milky bush," a green spiky plant, the white sap of which readily oozed out when broken and was supposed to blind a person. Like the forbidding fence at the Enrights, the one here at Vanhees had me wondering whether everyone was paranoid around here, or was I just naive? I had grown up in a house that didn't even have a key to its doors, much less a protective wall. It seemed so undignified to prepare one's house as if expecting robbers at any moment. And the crowning indignity was to be as we were now—completely at the mercy of a practical joker with a padlock. Why, with the spikes in the gate and the broken glass set into the wall, I would be hard put to escape from that yard bodily even if my life depended on it. So how much more unmanageable was the problem of getting that car out onto the street and on its way to the Zambian border before sundown!

Wrapped in dark thoughts, Robby got out what tools he had in the trunk of the car and began to try to cut the lock off. Thirty minutes passed thus, unfruitfully. I sat on the steps with Bismarck's cool nose resting on my knee. Bees buzzed in the shower of golden rain flowers hanging in their cloud above my head. I watched a rainbow lizard scuttle along the edge of the steps and disappear under the curled elephant ear leaves. What would be wrong with staying right here for two weeks instead of "doing Africa"? Maybe John and Harold had a point to make by locking us in. I had just traveled eight thousand miles and had found what I was looking for, so what was the big rush about getting on the road toward unknown destinations?

Thinking I might voice this opinion, I walked over to see Robby's progress on the huge padlock. The lock was still as firm as ever, and so was the determination on his face. Suddenly I knew I wouldn't say a word about canceling the trip. After all, it was Robby who had spent two years in this town and was ready for a break. It was Robby who had struggled to obtain visas, permits to leave the country, and reservations in the national parks of Zambia and Rhodesia. It was Robby who had pitted all his creativity against the hopeless state of the ransacked Dodge Dart. It was Robby who had overcome all my doubts about coming to Africa to marry him. A simple padlock was not going to cancel our honeymoon.

"How's it going?" I asked.

"Slow," he answered, straightening up to rest his back for a moment. "Oh, Susan, look," he said quietly, motioning with his chin to the street before us. Here came a troop of boys running with short quick steps, pushing before them the most ingenious little wire contraptions I had ever seen.

"They've used generator wire, unwrapping it from a junked car, then they've twisted and bent it to come up with a replica of some kind of vehicle. See, they have little steering wheels up at waist level; a long stick connects the steering wheel to the wheel base; then they run them over the ground on working wheels."

The curious boys ran close to the gate, guiding their prize productions absently by us while they tried to figure out what Robby was doing. Breaking in, they knew about. Breaking out was something new!

"Take a look," Robby said. I looked again at the fleet of wire vehicles poised with their proud chauffeurs before the closed gate. "Can you recognize any of the cars?"

I picked out the boy with the proudest grin and then looked down at his model. Sure enough, it was a Volkswagen bug, an exact replica of the car Robby and John Pannabecker had been using for the last two years. Not only was the familiar "bug" outline perfect, but there were the unmistakable wire lines copying the white racing stripes that ran off-center the length of the vehicle.

"*C'est bien!*" I exclaimed to the mimic artisan, wishing I knew his language; then, embarrassed, the boys skittered off like a herd of frisky colts, the little wheels glittering as they rolled over the pitted road.

"Maybe we should sneak out and get the Volkswagen back from John to use on our honeymoon," I half-jokingly suggested. "And leave him to get this car out himself."

"It is a good little car," said Robby, "but I wouldn't even consider taking a long trip in it. It's so easy to steal. That VW has been stolen at least six times since I've been in Lubumbashi. We'd get it back, eventually, minus gas, minus battery, minus tires. That's because I had put racing stripes on it. People around town got to know us in that car, and if they saw it abandoned somewhere outside of town, they'd come and let us know the next morning. Anybody could force open a window and hot-wire the thing in nothing flat. I wouldn't feel safe traveling in it," Robby finished. "I certainly wouldn't want our honeymoon ruined by having the car stolen when we're in some strange country hundreds of miles from anywhere."

Well, I'd have no more to say about the blue Volkswagen. Though I would have preferred to think that all this talk about theft was just paranoid, I remembered how many of Robby's letters in the past twenty-four months had begun with, "Well, they stole the car again last night, but we got it back today."

Picking up a file to keep chiseling away at the stubborn padlock, Robby saw a man come out of a house several doors down the street. He dropped the file. "I think that man's a mechanic!" he said, and began shouting to him. The man looked back at Robby as though he were crazy. Finally, though, he lit a cigarette and strolled over to our gate.

French was the native tongue of neither Robby nor this Greek mechanic. There was a great deal of misunderstanding just at first.

"So you've lost your key. . . ."

"No, actually, my friends have locked me in and taken the key, and I'd like to get out and start off on our honeymoon."

"You can't find your key?"

"No, it's not that. It's just that my friend put this padlock on, and I have no way of cutting it."

"But why would someone do that?" Evidently Greeks weren't familiar with American-style practical jokes.

Finally, forgetting explanations, Robby just worked on persuading the man to cut that padlock. Eventually, the man shook his curly head and went home for his tools. As he cut through the chain, he looked around him more than once, as if there was some lingering suspicion that perhaps he was illegally letting some outlaws escape.

Thanking our benefactor with relief, but not lingering a moment longer than necessary, we at last opened the gate and drove out, freed from our lovely prison. As we drove off down Avenue des Usines, I looked back to see the Greek man standing there watching us disappear into the distance as if he had just awakened from a puzzling dream. Robby noticed something else—the nonchalant figure of Harold Amstutz coming around a street corner swinging something that looked like a key on a chain. We found out later that Harold had followed us to Lubumbashi the night before in his airplane, determined to dog our footsteps. We had apparently escaped just in time to avoid any triumphant gloating on his part as well as possible new indignities.

There are no suburbs to Lubumbashi. One moment, you are in one of the largest cities in the country, and the next you are hemmed in on each side of the one paved lane of highway by tall elephant grass and the red peaks of termite "mountains." Some of the hills were shaped like small columns, just knee-high and rounded on the top like guardrails on a mountain curve. You'd break your foot before you'd kick it over, Robby said, tempting though it might be to try. Road builders crushed up those termite mounds to use as roadbed material, so well did those insects know their art.

I had looked at the map of Africa so many times that once we were on the road I could feel the car heading straight down the map toward the south, toward the Kasumbalesa border crossing into Zambia.

The bouquet of red wedding roses had shrunk now to a small spray that I had tucked at a dashing angle over my sun visor where I could breathe their warm perfume. Happiness spread through me like a ray of the sun that was toasting those roses through the windshield. The sign that the little Mickey Mouse radio had squawked to me in Brussels two years before had led me right. Thinking warm thoughts, I curled my legs up on the seat beside me and began singing. Robby's eyes met mine, then turned back to the road just in time to swing the wheel and miss a chameleon that was jerking across the road in its ancient, dirt-colored skin. I saw it just before it disappeared under the car like some miniature prehistoric dinosaur, the plastic kind you get in cereal boxes. A chameleon's ability to camouflage itself was distinctly disadvantageous while crossing a paved road, and I didn't imagine that many of the travelers along the way would swerve as violently as Robby did to miss the little reptile.

"I had one for a pet last year," he said. "He was such a cute little fellow. I'd just take him around the house to eat flies off the screens. If he got scared, he'd swell up and get hideous black spots. If I put him on my big philodendron, he'd turn grass-green. Once I put him on black iron window bars to catch mosquitoes, and when I came back I almost couldn't find him. He had turned as black as a bar of iron."

"How did you lose him?" I asked.

"He had crawled into my desk drawer, and when I opened it, it broke his back," he said regretfully. "But keep your eyes open, because if you see another nice one on the road, we could pick him up and take him home."

"Maybe on the way back," I said tactfully. "I mean, there aren't that many bugs in the car to feed him, and besides, he might get this nice clean car dirty." That should convince him. There was nothing Robby liked better than a clean car, not even reptiles. I had discovered that while loading the car for the trip. When *my* family traveled, we felt that the more pillows, books, pretzel bags, and pocketbooks crammed into the back window, the better. It was a real trip if, when Daddy stopped for a stoplight, Anita's doll and a couple of apples fell about your ears or water sloshed out of the container of flowers you were supporting between your feet. But when I suggested to Robby that we put the wedding cake box up in the back window where he could reach for it when hunger pangs struck, I encountered a decided no. Everything, even our sweaters, had to be locked up in the trunk. The only sign that we were travelers was the spray of roses dangling in front with the unmistakable aura of a wedding about them.

As we drove along, my mind drifted back to the day before the wedding, when Robby had gone eagerly to meet the weekly diplomatic flight from Kinshasa to Lubumbashi. His whole family was to have been on that flight, just in time to join in the wedding festivities. When the plane landed, and no Baxters materialized, Robby had climbed inside it and looked in every nook and cranny, refusing to accept that they were not there. But it was true.

Robby had been terribly disappointed that day and later that night when the bad news had been confirmed by ham radio. After all, he hadn't seen his mother and stepfather for years, as well as his sister Debby and brothers Jim and Bill, all in high school. The family had worked hard for weeks, securing visas and passports, submitting to one immunization after another, packing for a family of five, and then driving from Virginia to Anderson Air Force Base in South Carolina, where, as retired military personnel, they had the privilege of flying space available on an Air Force jet that was going to Monrovia and on to Kinshasa a few days before our wedding. That would have left them time to catch the weekly diplomatic flight to Lubumbashi, and there would have been some loved and familiar faces at our wedding.

Unfortunately, when already on board, the Baxters were told that all civilian passengers must deplane. Due to the nature of the cargo, they were not allowed on this flight after all. Stunned, they got off and stayed there for hours after the plane had taken off with its dangerous cargo. Mother was sure that it would return for them, but it continued on to accomplish its questionable mission, and the family went back to Virginia, missing the first marriage in their family.

"I'm sorry your family didn't make it to the wedding, Robby," I said.

"I'm sorry, too," said Robby. "I would love to show my sister and brothers Africa, and be with Mother and Dad again. But when you think about it, we might have had two days with them before the wedding, and then we would have been off on this honeymoon. What would they have done on their own?"

I hadn't thought of that. I assumed, I guess, that we would have hung around Lubumbashi a bit longer and done our traveling after they left, or—the Dodge Dart was a pretty big car, and they would certainly love to see Victoria Falls, too. I mean, one of the seven wonders of the world, and all that.

But Robby continued. "Because I wasn't going to take the five of them on this honeymoon, that's for sure. I've been waiting all my life to get you off by yourself." Then he laughed. "I guess I'd have deserved it, though, having been the third party on *their* honeymoon! I was four years old when Mom married Jim Baxter, and they included me on their wedding trip."

"It looks like you've been spared their revenge," I laughed with him.

We drove on, and Robby seemed to get sober and thoughtful again. We must be nearing the border, I thought. Was he apprehensive about that?

"What are you thinking about?" I asked finally.

"Oh, I've just been thinking about my other father," he answered. "I just have a shadowy memory of the person who met me at airports and took me to the movies or the zoo, and then dropped out of my life. I wonder about him a lot. Right now I wish I could find him, walk up and say, 'Here's Susan, my wife.' I really wish I could do that."

I was taken by surprise. Robby had never talked about his father. Jim Baxter was his Dad in every way, even lending Robby the Baxter name until at the age of eighteen, Bob Baxter chose to take the name he had been given at birth, Robert Wayne Ackerman

71

II. I knew that Bob Ackerman and his wife, Dorothy, were divorced when Robby was two years old, and that Robby had last seen his father at the age of four.

"Maybe someday we can go see him," I suggested. "Do you know how to look him up?"

"I don't even know if he's alive," Robby answered. "No one's heard of him for so long."

"Do you think he's dead?" I asked.

Robby was quiet for another stretch of highway. "No," he said finally. "I think he's changed his name and is living in some bizarre, out-of-the-way place doing something strange, but I don't think he's dead. And somehow I really think he'd be happy to meet his new daughter-in-law."

"Who knows?" I said out of the contentment that makes every dream within easy reach. "We'll probably run into him some day. After all, who would have believed two years ago that you and I would be here today in this car together, heading toward a honeymoon at Victoria Falls? Anything can happen!" The world was before us, but first, the border crossings.

7
Crossing the Border

We came up on the Kasumbalesa border without much warning. No town. Nothing but a rundown bar off to the right, nearly hidden by tall grasses. The only sign that we had come to the Congo's southern limit was a slim red-and-white striped pole resting on supports horizontally across the narrow road. We stopped in front of it. Robby opened his briefcase and got out our travel documents.

"I hope these laissez-passer papers won't look suspicious," he said. "You know I had gone by the immigration office in town so many times asking for these papers that allow us to leave the country, and they were always out of forms. So one day I typed up a laissez-passer form, ran off a thousand copies, gave five hundred copies to the immigration office, and kept five hundred for our own use. They were surprised, but I did get my travel papers stamped by the next day."

I followed Robby up to the door of the little office by the road. A flock of chickens scratching in the dust squawked and scattered at our approach. I could whiff the sour, starchy smell of something bubbling over a fire to the rear of the building, and I caught a glimpse of women relaxing on grass mats under a mango tree. One was wrapping thin black thread around a section of the hair of another, in an intricate design that must have taken all day to do.

As we hesitated at the door of the empty office, a young man in a bright white shirt strolled over to me. "You like my kitchens?" he said genially.

"Kitchens?" I looked wildly around to the black, bubbling pot out back—the nearest thing to a kitchen I could see.

"Yes," he said proudly. "These my kitchens." He waved in the direction of the poultry now attacking the rice-siftings that someone had thrown out on the neatly swept red dust.

"Oh, your chickens!" I said. "Your chickens are very nice! And you speak English!" I thought of how in a few weeks I would have my chance to improve the English of the young Congolese in Lubumbashi at least. Kitchens, indeed. I saw myself standing before an appreciative audience of teenagers eager to learn how to say *chicken* the way it should be said.

"Thank you," the young man said. "My kitchens are very fine, yes?"

"Yes, they are," I said.

Just then a portly official entered the room, wiping his mouth with the back of his hand. He and Robby exchanged the proper greetings and got down to business. The man took his time examining each document, but especially the mimeographed laissez-passer sheets. The visas in our passports merited a long look as well, and I held my breath as I remembered that Robby's passport had one extra entry into the Congo stamped upon it. Luckily, the fat passport with its extra pages falling out like an accordion to accommodate his frequent border crossings was familiar enough to this gentleman that he never stopped to match up exits, entries, and their respective dates.

74

He tossed the packet of papers on the table at last and made a gesture of finality. "But!" He leaned forward suspiciously. "I shouldn't have let you pass, you know."

Robby and I watched him warily, saying nothing.

"Don't think I didn't notice, just because I'm letting you pass."

"I'm not sure I understand," said Robby politely.

The man went on in a low voice. "I know very well that you typed up that laissez-passer yourself."

Robby was surprised. "It's just like the others," he protested.

"No, it's not," he insisted. "There are no typographical errors and no strikeovers. It's obvious that you did it yourself."

Smothering our amusement, we thanked him and returned to the car. The boy in the white shirt raised the striped pole, and off we went through the bush, the no-man's land between the Congolese immigration post and the customs stop ahead.

Then there were the same two stops to be made in Zambia, once we had entered that country. Things immediately seemed crisper and more prosperous. At Zambian immigration, we handed our passports to the uniformed man in charge. He paged through them carefully and courteously, then suddenly he stopped. He frowned. He looked up to scrutinize our two faces and checked to make sure that they really were the grim gray faces of the passport photos. Then he shook his head incredulously.

"This lady is your wife?" he asked in clipped African-British English.

"Yes," Robby answered, adding, "just since yesterday," as if that fact might be in his favor.

"But I don't understand." The man looked at the

two of us suspiciously. "How can that be possible? She is *older* than you."

Older! Just eleven months older, I thought in exasperation. He didn't need to have me tottering on the edge of the grave.

"Well, yes, you're right. She is older," Robby admitted.

The man reflected a moment, then called to the other men in the room, who came over to gawk at the passports and the two guilty culprits, as well. There were incredulous smiles and boisterous comments—probably not complimentary—in their native tongue.

At last Robby rose to the occasion. "It's all right, sir," he said. "My wife *is* older than me, it's true. But you see there was no one who wanted to marry her, and I couldn't find a younger girl who would come out to the Congo and marry me. So we ended up with each other. You know how it is, sometimes you just have to take what you can get." He looked apologetic. I tried to affix a properly humble expression to my face—the grateful, aging leftover who had been so nobly rescued by this self-sacrificing youth.

We rode into the prosperous mining town of Kitwe just after sunset. Not having had a decent meal all day, Robby had something on his mind.

"Before we go to the cottage, let's get a hamburger! There's actually a drive-in here where you can get hamburgers and grilled cheese sandwiches. In Lubumbashi no one's even heard of such things," Robby said. "I'll get a bag of them to go, and then we can have the leftover ones for breakfast."

For breakfast? I realized that I was getting a glimpse of the seamier side of bachelor life, but wasn't really in a position to offer any alternatives.

With a grease-spotted bag of what was to be our supper and breakfast, we drove through the lovely grounds of Mindolo Ecumenical Center and up to the edge of a lake where the Methodists maintained a guest cottage for travelers. While Robby unloaded the car and locked it up to his satisfaction, I lit a candle and spread out our evening meal. The candle's soft shining lent a certain beauty to the unfamiliar room and made it our home for the night.

Robby attacked the hamburgers seriously. As for me, I had my doubts. They looked nothing like hamburgers I had so recently seen—light, soft sesame seed bun warm and melting around the tender, saucy meat, crisp lettuce, and tomato. This roll was hard, dry, and tasteless, slathered with a runny mayonnaise, and it parted to reveal a hard lump of charred minced meat.

"Real hamburgers!" Robby said again, as he took another bite. I hoped he would devour the whole bagful, because I knew I could never face that sight the first thing in the morning.

Later, spreading the bed with the coarse cotton sheets we had brought with us, I admired the softness of the blue color and the daintiness of the embroidery on the top sheet. They were a gift from Mary Ruth and Pat, back in Lubumbashi, and were already special because they had been made of cotton grown in the Congo and not imported from Belgium or South Africa. While I was admiring the change the fresh sheets made in the little bedroom, Robby was tinkering with the lock on the window. He was beginning to make me nervous.

"Here, on the grounds of a church center, you still need to be constantly thinking about thieves?" I asked him.

He laughed. "One night Ken Enright left his pants and shirt hanging over this chair right here. His wallet was in the pants pocket. The next morning everything was gone. Somebody with a long arm had reached right through this window while he and Lorraine were sleeping." He stretched out on the bed, satisfied with the tight lock. "The funny part came the next day when Ken didn't have any clothes to put on and no money to buy new ones in town!"

I laughed, too, but took the precaution of sliding my open suitcase under the bed. The creamy, blue-trimmed negligee Nancy and Jan had given me, the lovely bridal slip, the heaps of matching, rainbow-hued undergarments—each one had been a gaily wrapped shower gift full of wishes for a happy marriage. I wasn't about to see them go the way of Ken's pants and shirt.

Trying to picture myself going into town the next morning and begging for clothes, I decided that, given the choice, I'd rather not. However, as things turned out, the next few days held a few other activities that I'd have preferred not to endure. In Ndola, I sat in a dreary garage redolent of diesel fuel and gasoline while the car was unhurriedly fitted with a fifth lug nut on each of its improvised wheels, as well as on the spare tire. I could understand getting the spare tire in tiptop shape, headed as we were for the wilds of the game parks, but if we had gone this far on four lug nuts a wheel, was it really necessary to install a fifth?

A garage is one of Robby's very favorite places, and he passed the afternoon quite pleasantly, watching and helping with the work, talking cars with the owner of the station. I was tempted to ask why he had gone to the trouble to import a bride, when it seemed as though all his needs were being met—for that afternoon, at least—by the car and the highly interesting activities in the Ndola garage.

The next day in Lusaka was even worse. To complete my yellow international health card, I needed a typhus vaccination, something I had been unable to get in Virginia in the weeks before I left the States. Hot and feverish for the rest of the day and the whole night long, I began to dream of our next stop—Victoria Falls. Since arriving on this continent, I had not seen even a wisp of a cloud in the sky, nor a drop of rain. I wanted to lose myself in the mists and rainbows of the giant waterfall.

8
The Smoke that Thunders

Niagara Falls had always been far down my list of possible honeymoon spots. What effect was all that rushing water supposed to have on a new marriage, anyway? But Victoria Falls was a different matter altogether. Victoria Falls is classed with the Grand Canyon and five other natural phenomena as one of the Seven Wonders of the World. Imagine being the only visitor to the Grand Canyon on a given day, having its splendor all to oneself. That's a little how we felt coming upon the elephantine Zambezi River—one mile wide—at the spot where it plunges 350 feet into a deep narrow chasm. It was like all of an ocean suddenly funneling itself back into a river of which the bottom had dropped out. The traditional African name for the falls is "The smoke that thunders," referring to the mysterious mist that cloaks the panorama so that only tantalizing patches of the mighty cascade can be seen at once. Like God, I suppose, keeping his back turned to Moses, so that the glory wouldn't be overwhelming.

Before we had ever discussed our own marriage, Robby had told me that he wouldn't marry unless he was in a position to give his wife a Paris honeymoon, if that was what she wanted. Well, he had more than lived up to his ambition. Any number of tourists and honeymooners might be climbing the Eiffel tower on a mid-July day at the height of the season, but Zambia had only just initiated its "See Zambia" campaign, and so far there weren't many takers. We had the falls and the park's rondavel facilities almost to ourselves.

Our third day of travel had brought us to Zambia's southern border town, Livingstone. As we drove out of town toward the falls, I caught a glimpse of the blue Zambezi river through the palm trees to the right of the highway. A caution sign along the road casually sported a picture of a hippopotamus, and another of an elephant, as if such huge beasts were as common and everyday as leaping deer on a Virginia mountain highway.

"Are they for real?" I asked Robby. "Or are they trying to make it exciting for tourists?"

He laughed at my naïveté. "I can tell you a story about how real they are. Last year, when I took my vacation, I wanted to see the falls before I did anything else. I got off a plane in Livingstone, and at the airport I didn't see much in the way of tourist information except a brand-new van that had "Zambia in the Sun" emblazoned across it in orange letters. It appeared that, for a fee, you could catch a ride to the falls, walk around admiring the view for a while, and then be chauffeured back to town to a hotel. I didn't see any alternatives, so I paid my kwacha, found a seat, and thirty minutes later I was at the falls. The several hours they allotted for seeing the falls didn't seem like enough time to me, so when the van was ready to head back to town, I decided to rent one of those little round camping huts for the night. The sunset was beautiful, and then the moon came out and made its famous circular rainbow down in the gorge of the falls. I climbed out on a rock projection to sit and think romantic thoughts with all that rainbow mist below me."

"That's sweet, but I thought this story was supposed to have something to do with elephants and hippos," I prompted him.

"I'm getting to it," said Robby reproachfully. "About ten o'clock that night I walked back to my hut and saw that there was a lantern lit at the one beside it. A man was sitting in the doorway. He was exhausted, he said, from helping at the scene of an accident. 'A bad one?' I asked. 'Bad enough,' he answered. 'A tourist van going 60 miles per hour slammed broadside into a hippopotamus waddling across the road. Nobody was killed, though, least of all the hippo. He just lumbered off and disappeared into the river. But all the people were taken to the hospital.' I asked him if that van happened to be wearing a 'Zambia in the Sun' banner—the one I should have been on. It was."

"Okay, so these hippo signs are for real. I believe you!" I kept my eye on the bushes and trees between our car and the river.

The park on the Zambian side of the Zambezi featured clean thatched-roof rondavels for rent. Each hut was furnished with two narrow cots and a tiny kerosene refrigerator, since there was no electricity. It was fun to unpack to play house Africa-style. But Robby was in a hurry to show me this river he had so fallen in love with. "When we registered at the office," he said, "I noticed a sign about a boat tour of the river upstream from the falls. It leaves about sunset, and I think we have just time to catch it."

Upstream from the falls? The ones that plunge to a

350-foot depth along a mile of precipice? I didn't have much interest in being in that situation no matter how beautiful it was at sunset.

"Is it—would it be safe?" I ventured.

Robby ignored the question as unworthy of me, and in a short time we were standing on shore at the launch site. I couldn't believe what I saw. There was a 100-ft. sightseeing boat, all equipped with benches and awnings. It was departure time for the Evening Special. (Zambia in the Sunset, perhaps?) I didn't see a single other sightseer on hand. Five Zambians lounged around near the engine.

"They probably won't want to go with just a 2-kwacha payload, will they?" I asked hopefully. "I don't mind putting off this excursion till another day."

But the crew was already starting up the engines. Maybe two passengers were two more than usually showed up. We walked across the gangplank, they drew it up, and we slowly pulled through the little palm-lined inlet out onto the deceptively smooth bosom of the great Zambezi.

After the heat of the day's travel, the cool evening breeze felt wonderful. We headed west—upstream, thank goodness, toward the gold-washed sunset sky. The guide roared above the noise of the engine that up this way there were islands with elephants and hippos. If it weren't for the noisy and vibrating deck of the tour boat under my feet, I'd have felt cut off from all signs of civilization. Downstream, when I dared to allow my glance to linger, I could see clouds of spray billowing up from where the water took its fantastic plunge. The mist mounted high in the sky like a mushroom sign of disaster emanating from some new and powerful sort of energy. Upstream, and on either side of us, papyrus swamps led into dense tangled jungle scenes. Once, on a sandbar, an elephant tossed his heavy head and flapped his ears in an annoyed way at the noise of our motor, in much the same way a man might try to escape the whine of a mosquito in his ear.

At the edges of another island, long, sausage-like ovals lined up in the water signaled the communal bathing place of three or four submerged hippos, only the top of their backs visible.

Gold deepened to rose and then purple, and the launch turned back toward the inlet. The wind whipped my hair, and suddenly I was glad we were the guests of honor on the Zambia Sunset Special. I looked sideways at Robby, who, with his photographer's eye, was judging just when to snap another sky picture for a new color effect.

"Fun!" I shouted through the noise of the engines. "And it doesn't look like we'll be swept over the falls after all!"

On the way back to the park, Robby told me about the time he *had* nearly been swept over a waterfall here in the Congo. "It was the most terrible feeling. John and I were floating down a river near Kapanga, when suddenly the current felt swifter, and I heard the noise of falling water echoing from a long way down. Quickly turning from a lazy float into a hurried crawl for the shore, I couldn't make any headway.

John was closer to shore and managed to pull out of the current into calmer water and eventually reach the riverbank. I saw a rock poking out of the water and strained to reach it as the drag of the water pulled me away. I just made it and pulled myself up to perch on its narrow safety. I sat . . . and sat . . . and sat. I just couldn't get up the courage to plunge back into that water. I was so close to the drop that I could see water shooting over, but I couldn't see a bottom. John tried to be helpful, reaching out to me with branches and whatever else he could find. But the distance was too great. Finally John went for a rope, and I worked my way to the riverbank holding on to it. That's as close as I ever want to be to a waterfall from upstream."

"I'm glad you didn't write all these stories to me," I said when he had finished. "It was enough to hear about ears being nailed to the post office walls and the public hangings, not to mention the rampage of soldiers through the province. If I had to worry about run-ins with nature as well, I would have really been nervous."

"Just wait," he teased. "I have more stories."

"Well, I'm here with you now," I said.

"To keep me from going over Victoria Falls in an empty 100-foot launch?"

"Of course! Someone in the family has to be sensible!"

Most of this honeymoon trip we were to rely on fruit and bread and cheese for our picnic lunches wherever we happened to be, topped off with slices of the dehydrating but ever-present wedding cake—for Robby, that is. But this night we would dine at the riverbank restaurant in style.

Digging out long-sleeved pullovers against the evening chill of winter in the Southern Hemisphere, we dressed and set out along a sandy moonlit path that trailed along the river under giant palm fronds and cypress-like trees to where a string of colored lights announced food, drink, and festivities. As we walked, gnarled roots exposed above the sand looked enough like waiting crocodiles stretched out in the darkness to give me an unpleasant shiver.

We hadn't been seated long in the dimly lit dining room before it became obvious from the raised voices that there were fellow Americans in the room.

"Moo—see—uh—tun—how does it go? Oh, your names are just impossible to say. As bad as some of our Indian names. I think Victoria Falls sounds a lot more sensible!"

Before the long windows overlooking the river was a table for six. Five women in various shades of hot pink and mauve and aqua with hair tinted to match were leaning toward a tall, young Zambian who sat ramrod straight. It was obvious that he was their guide, and not very comfortable with the whole affair.

"No, no, Evelyn; we've got to know how they say it, so when we show our slides back home we can show a picture of the falls and tell them the real African name. It's here in this travel brochure: Moo-see-oh-tune—tell me again, Benjamin."

Another voice broke in: "You don't mind if we call you just plain Benjamin, do you? Your other name is simply impossible. Oh, thank you; you're a dear."

"Won't you have something more to drink, Benjamin? Beer, a cocktail, wine? Waiter, another martini for everyone. Nonsense, Benjamin, you *must* have another. *We're* paying the bill, you know. The treat's on us, as we Americans say!"

The voices seemed to get louder and louder. And the young man, whose replies were inaudible, appeared more and more uncomfortable. I was embarrassed to identify myself with the nationality of these tourists, though, fortunately, at the moment they and we were the only diners in the restaurant.

"Well, Victoria Falls *is* more magnificent than Niagara, though I can't help wishing you could see the whole mile of it all at once. It would make a more

86

impressive photograph," said one of the ladies.

"And just think!" broke in another. "The falls had been here all those centuries and not a soul laid eyes on it until David Livingstone finally found it. Isn't that amazing! What a wonderful brave man he must have been."

I gulped to keep from shouting that of course a great number of Africans had seen the falls before David Livingstone. There was a pause as Benjamin evidently made some kind of suggestion.

"Oh, no, no," one of them answered. "We don't really have the time to go into the Livingstone Museum."

"But, Goldie," another objected. "We should at least have the taxi stop by tomorrow and see if they have any pamphlets or anything about the museum. For our talks, you know."

"Oh, you're right, Ethel. Just like you were right about bringing Lysol Spray and our own supply of soft toilet paper." They all giggled. "You can hardly call some of this stuff you find toilet tissue. It's more like crepe paper, or newspaper, or waxed paper, and it's such a horrid gray."

Robby leaned toward me and whispered, "I haven't traveled many places in Africa where they even had rest rooms, much less toilet paper of any kind!"

Just then the waiter came past them carrying our salads, and all six heads turned in our direction.

"Look at that sweet little couple!" one of them stage-whispered. "I wonder if they live in this backward country, bless their hearts. Or maybe they're traveling like us."

Robby pushed back his chair. "I'm going over to talk to them." With his big innocent blue eyes and boyish blond hair, he had a way of especially appealing to the over-60 crowd. Though I couldn't hear

Robby's soft voice, some of theirs certainly carried across the room:

"Teaching them *what?* Two young men teaching two hundred women to cook and sew and wash their babies? Listen to that, Ethel! How wonderful! And now your wife will help, too. It is so noble of you. And what a sacrifice! Where did you say this city was?"

"Lu-Lu— Well, I don't think it's on our itinerary. You know, we just have fifteen days, and we'll be doing the pyramids of Egypt, the Serengeti in East Africa, shopping in Johannesburg—that's South Africa, isn't it?—and I forget what else."

Another voice broke in: "Of course we're Presbyterian, not Methodist, but when we get home, we'll see if there's any work in Lu-Luman—in your town. And if there is, we'll give a donation!" she finished triumphantly.

Breakfast was better. Traveling in a country influenced by the British Empire, I find breakfasts are always better. You're sitting there with a pot of tea tucked under a knitted cozy, and little bowls of chilled butter, and marmalade, and racks of toast, and a savory plate of eggs and ham with grilled mushrooms and tomatoes on the side—and, besides that, the whole day is before you. Robby was learning to be patient as I drank tea for both of us. He usually dispatched a glass of milk or juice and attacked the eggs seriously. I was discovering, with a sense of betrayal, that breakfast to him was only a matter of taking in fuel for the morning. At this point in our days-old marriage, though, he was indulgent with me.

"Another cup?" he asked, and I nodded. I was never sure if the extra pot of hot water was intended to be used to dilute the first pot if I found it too strong, or to make a second pot of tea with the used leaves of the first pot. I took a chance on the latter, since I had already drained the first pot of tea single-handedly.

This was our day for a trek through the Rhodesian side of the falls. There was a long trail following the edge of the Falls in several different directions through a rain forest. Robby was planning to find some photogenic angles, and his mind was already on his camera and film supply.

Finally, unable to sip another sip, I folded my big white linen napkin and announced that I was ready for the day. Outside the restaurant, we got into the car to drive to where the trail began.

"Need to do anything else before we start out?" I asked, the thought crossing my mind that a visit to the rest room might not be a bad idea after all that tea. "Need anything back at our room?"

"No, I'm ready to start," he answered. "I've got everything I need in my camera bag." He seemed to be single-minded about this hike around the falls. "Shall we go?"

How long would this walk be, anyway? I wondered. If I didn't find a bathroom soon, it could get uncomfortable. Well, *he* would certainly have to go sometime, and I didn't feel like being the one to bring it up, not when he seemed so set on going ahead.

We drove through the park headquarters, through the rondavel sites, and were just getting to the road when I saw a sign "Ladies" and "Gents" in a building that seemed to house public showers.

"Oh, look over there," I said brightly. "Rest rooms!"

Robby didn't look in the direction I indicated. He kept driving ahead with an absorbed look on his face.

"Did you realize that tea is a diuretic?" I tried again. "And I certainly finished off the pot this morning all by myself. Thoughtful of them to have these rest rooms placed so well between breakfast and the falls!" I stopped chattering long enough to realize that he wasn't paying the slightest attention to a word I said. I turned to stare at him. His gaze was fixed on the road ahead, the morning sun slanting into his face and turning his blue eyes into clear sparkles of light.

He must have felt my eyes on him, and the silence, and maybe the tension that was beginning to rise. He blinked and came back to the present.

"What? Did you say something about tea? No, I didn't drink any tea this morning. My nose runs when I drink hot drinks. And caffeine really makes me keyed up. I took a No-Doz once in college and didn't sleep for three nights."

What this had to do with going to the bathroom, I did not know. What was crystal-clear to me was that he hadn't heard what I was saying at all. I began to boil inside. He had brought me all the way to Africa just to ignore me. So this was the way marriage really was. All those jokes about the husband hiding behind a newspaper while his wife chattered on used to be laughable. Never again. It looked like my husband could fit the stereotype perfectly even without benefit of a newspaper to hide behind. (Or did a steering wheel serve the same function?)

My thoughts flashed back to the two years just past, when I was free. I had my little burgundy-colored Peugeot 404, symbol of the gaiety and adventure of Bunni's and my trip to Europe, and I went when and where I pleased. Bunni—ah, there was a traveling companion who not only drank just as many cups of tea as I did but who also cooperated heartily in the search for rest rooms, or hedgerows in French wheat fields, as the situation called for. I was appalled at the new state of affairs. In just a matter of fourteen days I had been transformed from an employed woman who paid property taxes and managed a trip across three continents and a couple of oceans all by herself—to this humiliated chattel who sat in the passenger seat of this man's vehicle and, it appeared, would have to get down on her knees and *beg* for a privilege most people take for granted.

And that I would not do. I stared straight ahead and remained silent. From the sun visor dangled the limp wedding roses, now fading to brown.

To this day I remember but little about the Rhodesian side of the falls. It was the most "developed," the breakfasts were better, there were more tourists strolling around, the paths going out along the gorge were longer—or did it just seem so to me that morning? What I remember very well is the predictable effect of all that splashing, rushing water. Parents take advantage of that response to running water when they turn on a faucet to encourage the child who's being potty-trained. To me, such super-faucets that were thundering wantonly all around were sheer torture.

Spray dripped down over our heads and off our noses, beaded on our hair and fogged up the camera lens, a fact which preoccupied Robby's mental efforts. Thus he appeared totally unaware of *my* preoccupation. Well, I would definitely not hold his hand as we walked down the path. It was narrow anyway and wet on both sides, and I was feeling anything but companionable. But Robby never reached for my hand, so I was denied the pleasure of ignoring him.

Shots of wet-beaded grasses with only billows of mist behind, where the falls were hiding; shots of gnarled tree roots losing their grasp of ancient earth and flying free over the brink, with the angle just right to catch the fall's rainbow in the mist behind; shots of baboons, hiding in dense foliage and no doubt undetectable in the resulting photograph. The hours went by as the shutter clicked—in misery for me, too proud as I was to disappear around a palm tree for a few minutes.

It was twelve o'clock noon when our path led us back to the car and on to our rondavel to get ready for lunch—and, of course, the fight. I'd heard about these honeymoon fights. One couple I knew spent several totally silent days when the husband stuck a pin in a balloon his wife had asked him not to pop. Outrage for another new bride came on the second day of her marriage, when she looked over the menu at a beach restaurant and said luxuriously, "I think I'll have a milkshake." "Do you really think you need it?" the new husband asked. That started a twenty-four hour free-for-all. I suppose it was our turn, but first I'd go back to the room and freshen up.

We'd never had a fight before, so I wasn't exactly sure how I would go about it. I knew one thing. We had already put in our time being distant and lonely. Through the window I could see Robby laying out our picnic lunch meticulously on the lawn table. I could go out and run my hands through his hair. But, no, I was mad at him, though a visit to the rest room had already taken a lot of the oomph out of my resentment.

"Susan, come here!" At Robby's low but urgent call, I hurried out onto the lawn.

"Hi, fella," he said, holding out his hand, but not to me. A little greenish monkey was creeping steadily toward the picnic table, timid, but longing for the orange section Robby was offering. I walked closer at the same time, but she didn't seem to be taking any notice of me. She paused now and then to look back over her shoulder with a hangdog expression and then inch forward toward the succulent piece of fruit. Just as her tiny black fingers began to curve up to snatch it, there was a raucous clamor from the trees. A huge male bounded across the yard, hurling imprecations at the female, who had dropped the orange and was off like a shot to hide in the trees, whimpering and begging. The male, flashing his tacky red and blue rear end, bounded up, grabbed the orange, and ran back to where his mate was cowering. As he devoured the orange section, he lectured her loudly between bites. The female kept her eyes fixed hungrily and wistfully on the disappearing fruit.

"It could be worse," I muttered to myself.

"What did you say?" Robby asked, moving over to put his arm around me.

"Just that I'm glad I'm not *his* wife."

Robby was quiet for a moment, then said, "This morning I wasn't so sure you were enchanted with being mine, either."

It was my turn to be surprised. He *had* noticed. "Oh, that," I said. "Nothing wrong with me that a rest stop couldn't fix. What have you got to eat there? Besides wedding cake, I mean!"

9
Wankie's Wilds

Plains of sun-golden grass swept by the car, punctuated by spreading trees. We were on a wonderfully smooth and modern highway leading from Victoria Falls southward to the great game reserve called Wankie, tucked in Rhodesia's northwestern corner beside neighboring Botswana. Above us spread the great blue banner of Africa's dry season sky.

"This is the best time of year to view game," Robby commented eagerly as we neared the park. "During the summer rains there's so much vegetation that animals can hardly be seen. And they have no need to group around the watering holes in the evening, since water can be found everywhere."

"How do these game parks work?" I asked Robby nervously. "We just drive our car around anywhere in the park and hope to see some animals? Are they ever dangerous?"

How did I get into this anyway? High adventure had never been first on my list of life goals. Was it only five months ago that Jan and I sat in our tiny Harrisonburg apartment with our feet up on the kitchen table, knitting and watching the snow fall, while the cat purred, and the cozy wood fire snapped and crackled? We had talked about everything under the sun, except—why, certainly not the lure of tracking wild animals through the African bush. Any savage beasts we imagined were the two-legged kind.

"Here's the park entrance now," Robby said. "See, there's a high protective fence all around the rest camp and armed guards at the gate. When we leave the camp early tomorrow morning to drive through the game-viewing areas, we have to sign out. Then we must be back by six o'clock in the evening; if not, they'll come out looking for us."

Things didn't seem very dangerous that night as we sat down to a white linen tablecloth, scarlet flowers tucked into the folded napkin, and a full-course British meal of roast beef, Yorkshire pudding, and trifle. Within the encircling wire fence, there was every effort to make our stay comfortable and delightful, from the neatly kept cottages to the tree-sheltered dining room and the little store where we bought supplies for the next day's picnic in the park.

The meal ended with a small dish of fruit, several different varieties of melon, I guessed. But at the first bite, I knew it wasn't melon. I frowned.

"Robby, what is this?" I took a taste of the richer orange fruit, and frowned again. "It can't be cantaloupe!"

"It's not," he laughed. "You'll see a lot more of these fruits in the next year than you will cantaloupe."

I took another exploratory bite of the smooth, almost oily dark orange fruit. "This one tastes like a cantaloupe that's been crossed with honeysuckle," I decided. "I wasn't prepared for that flowery taste, but it's not so bad when you're expecting it."

"Papaya," Robby said.

"And the other one—" I took a bite of the firmer yellow one. "This one tastes like a peach that was

95

crossed with a pine tree."

"And that's mango," he said.

"Strange, but I think I could get used to them," I decided. I didn't know then that these two fruits could be addictive, and that years later in other climates I would dream of a papaya half, chilled, drenched in fresh lime juice—and just beyond my reach.

"I'm glad that at least the fruits were African," I said as we walked back to the cottage in the moonlight. "The meal was delicious, but so British, we could have been anywhere in the world. We should have had a bit of zebra, or some elephant curry."

"Or monkey?" Robby offered.

"Well, no, actually, I wasn't thinking of monkey," I shuddered.

"Neither was I one night out in the bush, but that's what the villagers brought me to eat." Robby laughed. "Actually, the monkey wasn't bad, seasoned with onions and tomatoes and eaten with big mouthfuls of rice. And it was an honor to be served meat in a village that rarely enjoyed that luxury. The only problem I had was the stinkbugs."

"Stinkbugs!"

"They had hung a lantern above me, and this attracted the bugs, which in turn fell down into the rice. I didn't want to appear rude, by spitting them out, so I had to chew very carefully around the bugs and swallow them whole. I missed once, and got a mouthful of that disgusting fluid. Otherwise, I'd say that monkey meat is quite acceptable, when you're hungry."

"Look at the moon," I said, linking my arm through his and changing the subject. "Remember how we used to always celebrate full moon nights by taking a walk together back in Virginia?"

Later in the night, I awoke to realize that the moon had other worshipers. Long, drawn-out shivering howls wound through the windows of our tiny cottage. There were snuffling, growling noises that seemed far closer than the high chain link fence should allow. I was actually trying to sleep here, surrounded by legendary savage animals on every side, hunting and killing in the light of the moon, for their survival and that of their cubs and kittens. It wasn't a thought to lull one into slumber, and I pulled the pillow over my head.

The moon had vanished, and the sun had taken its place to try to warm the dusty track before us as we signed out with the guard and started our drive through our chosen area of the park.

"Do not get out of your car under any circumstances," the guard had reminded us. "Picnic only in the fenced enclosures. If you have car trouble, wait, and someone will find you. And be sure to be back by six o'clock sharp. We don't want to go looking for you in the dark!"

The scrubby trees beside the road were heavy with a ruddy dust. The dry season might be great for viewing animals, but I wondered wistfully how this would all look in a driving, cleansing rain, bringing the dark greens and browns to velvety life, ready to catch the sun's sparkling rays after the storm. Robby's mind was still on the park official's warnings.

"You know, Susan, there was an American who came through here recently, hitchhiking. He got a ride with someone into the park, but at one of the picnic spots he got out to see if he could get some photographs, and the car went on. When his name wasn't crossed off that night as the cars came back in, they sent out a search party. He was lucky they found him—still alive, but barely. It appears that the cape buffalo doesn't like to have its picture taken at close range."

"How is a cape buffalo different from the American buffalo?" I asked.

"It's massive and black, with two huge curled horns, easily angered. It's one of the few animals that can kill a lion, not to mention hunters and hitchhikers. We're sure to see some today," he answered.

I eyed the metal frame of the car; it had never appeared to me so fragile and delicate.

We had been driving along the deserted park trail for some time, with no sign of an animal. This was going to be harder than I thought. There was something to be said for zoos, with animals lined up in their designated places. If you wanted to see a giraffe, all you had to do was follow the giraffe signs. And if you wanted to see a cape buffalo, you could press your nose against a very solid protective fence as you looked your fill.

Suddenly Robby made a soft exclamation and slowed the car. In the bush on both sides of us and littered over the road were the remains of someone's efforts to cut wood or clear brush. There was nothing very remarkable about it, only that whoever it was certainly hadn't cleaned up after themselves very well. There were leaves, branches, and broken twigs scattered over the road, and some of the trees alongside the road were stripped half bare. Jagged butts of branches jutted out of half-destroyed trees, and in some places, branches were twisted and stripped, but still hanging on the tree.

"This was breakfast," Robby said. "A troop of elephants had breakfast here. Look, the leaf litter is still fresh. They can't be far away."

I was awed. If this was breakfast, how could the forest sustain the assault of lunch and dinner, and tomorrow's elephantine meals as well?

The car wheels rolled and crunched over the rubble. In a few hundred yards, the bush opened up into a grassy plain, and there they were. There must have been a hundred elephants, moving as if indeed those tusks and heavy trunks were cumbersome baggage, and yet covering a surprising amount of ground in spite of their bulk. A tiny elephant child—tiny in the sense that a Volkswagen is tiny compared to a trailer truck—bounced and tripped along beside its mother, like a windup toy. She swung her trunk protectively his way as if to keep him securely in line, and he ducked to avoid it with the morning energy all babies spend against their mothers. Several elephants, as if to cleanse themselves of all traces of breakfast, tossed trunkfuls of rusty dust over their shoulders, with great flapping of ears and stomping of feet. We were totally ignored, our vehicle stopped in the middle of the road to watch the gigantic beasts move off the scene.

When they were gone, I drew a deep breath. "I changed my mind," I told Robby. "I don't think I'll ever want to go to a zoo again. Let's drive on. Do you think we'll see any lions?"

"They're hard to see because they sleep in the grass by day so they can hunt at night, but keep your eyes open."

Tantalized now, we made our way over the park trails the whole morning long. In a shady ravine, we came across crocodiles who had slithered up out of the small river to find spots of sun. They looked too lazy to be threatening.

"With jaws and teeth like that, who needs to look

energetic?" was Robby's assessment of their languor, and I looked again with more respect.

On the open plains, herds of various antelopes and gazelles moved across the grass as if sent before a gentle wind, heads raised at intervals to scent the air for enemies. A giraffe, at close quarters, tilted her head quizzically and regarded me with soft amused eyes, as if to say, You people look so funny crouched inside that purring case of metal, peering out at us.

Toward evening the animals rose and stretched after their afternoon naps and made their way to the watering holes. We came around a hill, and there before us were hundreds of cape buffalo taking turns drinking at the pool and using this opportunity to kick up a ruckus over an especially attractive female. Their sheer numbers were breathtaking, not to mention their imposing size. Birds found the massive shoulders a convenient place to perch after their evening drink, and it was a strange contrast in ferocity—the angry-looking buffalo head crowned by a flighty little sparrow.

"It's nearly five o'clock," Robby said, consulting his park map. "Let's take one last loop. It should get us back to the gate well before six."

We were going slowly through a small patch of forest, watching baboons scamper into the bushes at our approach and then turn around to hurl insults, when I noticed ahead of us another pile of litter.

"Elephants again?" I said aloud.

"It's a small pile; it could be a lone elephant," Robby said. He slowed the car, and we searched the trees on either side. The car wheels straddled a pile of elephant manure that could enrich the soil of an entire vegetable garden.

Then we rounded a curve in the trail, and there he

was, one lone bull, ripping a trunkful of leaves off a tree and blocking the road with his dusty gray bulk. Robby quickly brought the car to a stop, letting the engine idle.

The beast was unbelievably wrinkled. Skin hung in leathery folds, crisscrossed by lines in every direction. We watched as he efficiently gleaned what he wanted from the shrubs and trees and stuffed it down his throat, oblivious to our presence.

Or was he? Five minutes went by, and ten, and even though the elephant had stripped that tree, he remained in position across the road, effectively blocking our passage. He stood there, letting his trunk dangle and his tiny eyes glaze over, motionless. There was no way around him.

"Well, any time now, fella. . . . We're interested in getting on down the road," Robby said under his breath.

"What if we're late?" I worried. I noticed the car's engine skip a beat or two as it idled. "How long can the car keep idling without getting too hot or something?"

"Oh, it's okay so far," Robby said, watching that elephant. "Susan, I think he's doing this on purpose."

It certainly did seem so. There he stood, motionless, an immovable gray wall of flesh between us and our destination.

"What if he. . . ." I paused. I certainly didn't want to sound childish, but what if he decided to walk over and sit down on our car?

Just then, the elephant turned slightly toward us. The giant stumps of feet moved restlessly.

"That does it!" Robby said. "I'm going to back up. We'll never get around him, anyway, as long as he can help it. And we've got less than thirty minutes to check in at the rest camp."

Was that a glimmer of satisfaction in those dull elephant eyes as we slowly moved backward in our tracks? I hoped it was. We found a clearing where we could turn the vehicle around for a mad dash back to the camp just as the sun set and the park agents were checking their watches.

Three days passed at Wankie as we covered all the far reaches of the park. Though we eventually saw almost every possible African wild animal, the big cats eluded us. Not one lion, not a cheetah, not a leopard did we see.

"We'll have another chance when we get to the Matopos," Robby said, as we drove away from our little cottage that last morning.

"Wait!" I said suddenly. In the mirror I could see someone running wildly after us, waving something in his hand.

Robby brought the car to a stop to let the man catch up with us. It was evidently the person cleaning the room we had just vacated. From the veranda of the park office, several park visitors watched in amusement as the breathless man waved a scrap of blue lace in the air.

"Madam has left something among the linens!" he shouted for all to hear.

"How embarrassing!" I muttered as Robby accepted the forgotten item with great aplomb.

"Hey, it's a honeymoon!" he laughed and drove on, leaving the amused porch-sitters behind in a veil of red dust.

10
The Moon and the Matopos

The car went forward in thick blackness. We were still heading south, into what was Rhodesia at the time, now Zimbabwe, but at eight o'clock at night and with no lights to be seen in any direction, it felt very much as though we were falling off the map into a deep, dark hole. We had reservations for a rondavel in the Matopos National Park, but what good did reservations do us if we couldn't even find the place?

The park area didn't look *that* big on the map, not big enough to be totally and hopelessly lost in for hours. But we were apparently going in an endless circle, and there was an eerie quality to the night, almost as if the stars were being blotted out by a giant, sinister hand.

"There's something!" I saw a tiny sign by the side of the road, pointing out a government residence. "Maybe we can ask directions there."

Robby backed up, pulled into an uphill driveway, and got out of the car. Then he paused, uncertainly. There were loud shouts, and a door slammed. Somewhere inside, a woman began crying hysterically. Something crashed against the door, and then there was more shouting and crying.

Robby came back and got into the car. "I've just changed my mind," he said. "We can find that rest camp by ourselves—it's got to be around here somewhere. I don't really want to get involved in a domestic quarrel."

"Let's just go on," I agreed, just as dubiously.

The sounds of battle faded in the darkness behind us as we quickly got back on our way, not much encouraged. I wasn't sure if we were going in the same direction as we had been. In fact, I kind of hoped we weren't. The idea of ending up back among the lights and modern hotels of the city of Bulawayo sounded pretty good to me. Just as I was about to express this to Robby, he said, "Here we are."

Before long I could see, too, a pinprick of light ahead and to the left. We passed under an arched stone entrance, and the pinprick of light swayed toward us. It turned into a gas lantern swung by a tall dark man in an immense black greatcoat that hid his boot tops. He leaned into our car window as we stopped.

"Collinson?" he asked, consulting the one reservation paper on his clipboard.

"Yes, Collinson," Robby replied. I was startled and almost sputtered a little. Collinson? Whatever happened to Ackerman? Was Robby that tired of driving that he was willing to take someone else's reservations? Could this desolate camp really be that full?

"This way," the man directed, and we followed that lonely light down a deserted lane to the tiniest round hut imaginable. There was a hospitable glow in the window, and when we opened the door, we saw a cheery lantern burning from the rafters. I tried not to think of the Collinsons who might even now be driving in tired desperation toward their night's rest.

Chilled to the bone, we settled in. Our little gas camp stove had some hot tea steaming for us in no time. We had expected that there would be a small dining room at Matopos as there had been at the falls and Wankie. But there were no dining facilities and no hot dinner to be enjoyed by the fireplace. I searched through the plastic bag of edibles and found some cheese and crackers. They didn't quite fill the aching void.

"There's always cake," Robby said, brightening suddenly. "Could you cut me a slice?"

Out of our picnic cooler I took the no-longer-white-nor-square bakery box. It was crumpled and battered, and its red-brown color bore a telling resemblance to the color of the Wankie trails we had meandered over for three days. The interior was no better.

"It's ruined," I said firmly, tapping my middle finger on the hard dry hunk of leftover cake. "We've got to throw it out." The pastry was no longer an unappetizing gray but had blended with the red dust to form a sickly brown.

"Don't throw it out!" Robby said in horror.

"Look. It's nine days old, it's hard as a rock, and it's covered with dust."

"See if you can brush it off a little. Here. . . ." He took his handkerchief, and brushing and blowing until he was satisfied with the cake's appearance, gave me the honor of choosing my piece first.

"I told you I'm not eating any," I insisted. He may not have noticed, but I hadn't tasted a bite since the day we were married and didn't intend to start now that it resembled a kind of moon rock.

"By the way, just what do we do if the *Collinsons* show up and want this hut?" I asked as he prepared to enjoy his cake.

"The Collinsons?" He was genuinely puzzled.

"Yes, the Collinsons. I'd never heard the name before this evening, and I felt really uncomfortable when you told the man at the entrance that we were the Collinsons. Why couldn't you have told him who we really are? I feel uncomfortable knowing that we could be here without the right to be. Maybe it's my Mennonite upbringing, but I always have to explain the truth no matter how inconvenient it is. I'd rather be sleeping out in the dark car than taking someone else's place. Of course I know you and I are different, but I didn't think we were *that* different." I was getting wound up now and would have launched into chapter two except for the grin that was spreading over my husband's face.

It made me furious. "You laugh at me, do you? Well, I can't help it; that's the way I am, and you knew it very well when you married me."

"Wait a minute before you get all excited." He took a big bite of cake and chewed it slowly and maddeningly before he swallowed and grinned again. "I like it when you're really telling me off. But in this case, it's really not necessary. Don Collinson is a Methodist photographer who lives in Salisbury, Rhodesia, and he made the reservations for us in these parks in his own name. It was simpler to say yes, Collinson, than to explain who we really were."

I felt suddenly very foolish, but at the same time relieved. My husband was not a cold-blooded deceiver, but had his own logic to follow that I was unaware of. Still, I sighed. It would take time for us to pool our separate stores of knowledge and points of view so that we could really live in understanding.

"What I would have done is this." I thought I'd let him see how the other half thought. "I would have

106

leaned out the window and explained to that man with the lantern, that, no, we weren't the Collinsons, we were the Ackermans, but the Collinsons had made the reservations for us, the Ackermans. Therefore, the Collinson reservations were really for us, the Ackermans. Then everything would be clear to everybody. See?"

"This is Africa, Susan. The man wouldn't have understood English very well, and he would have somehow latched onto the fact that we weren't the Collinsons, and the hut was for the Collinsons, so he would have made us go into the office while he went to find his superior and figure out what was to be done with these Ackermans who had just showed up without reservations."

"And we would have been even colder by the time we got to bed," I agreed. "I guess I have some things to learn about surviving in Africa." Then as I started to clear away the tea things, another thought occurred to me. "Robby, we would have been spared this entire discussion if you had just told me who Don Collinson was."

A wicked grin spread over his face, and he reached out to hug me to him. "Yes, but aren't they fun, these discussions?"

I had to admit that being momentarily upset with Robby was much better than being eight thousand miles away from him. The thatched roof above us was cozy and, while the teapot was boiling, the little gas flame gave us an illusion of warmth. But now we could feel the cold creeping in around us. This was July, and to my Western mind it shouldn't be cold. But, well below the equator, we were actually doing our not-very-well-equipped camping in the dead of winter. My heaviest wrap was a hand-knit Irish fisherman sweater. It was decidedly not enough. By bedtime we were really shivering and there was no question of each using his own slender, saggy cot. We piled both sets of blankets on one and crawled in to enjoy the warmth of two in a cot. There wasn't much space for turning to get comfortable, that was for sure, but the shared body warmth began to sink into our bones and stop the shivering.

With the gas lantern turned off, that thick blackness pressed down on us again. This was nothing like a tropical night as I had already began to know it, birds arguing sleepily, crickets and frogs humming, cats prowling, the smoke from a night guard's fire mixing with the perfume of tangerine blossoms, and somewhere a drum beating softly, or a voice raised in a high, wild song to help pass the night.

But here in the Matopos at midnight, sound had frozen. I began to feel that I was on a different planet, on the sterile cold rocks of the moon, and I took an involuntary gasp of air. Yes, that was still oxygen, I supposed. Robby was asleep, exhausted with all the driving and searching. I was wide awake, if the word wide could be used in reference to a person confined to such a small place. I shifted my position as best I could to get my arm—numb as a log—out from under Robby's head. No, we were no longer eight thousand miles apart, nor was I very comfortable.

Robby seemed to be sleeping just fine. I rested against his chest and tried to calm myself into sleep. Then I was aware of a low, steady sound in my ear. His heart was beating. "Lub. . . ." pause "a-dub," it went. Why was that little pause in there? I wondered. Weren't hearts supposed to say "lub *dub*" or something like that? Shouldn't the pause be between the "dub" and the next "lub?" I listened carefully, all my nerves atingle. The heart beat on, but always after that first "lub," there was a tired pause that made me think his heart was actually debating whether to go on with it or not.

He was lying so still and quiet. Could he be sick? I knew he had survived polio and a kind of tuberculosis and had narrowly escaped having a tracheotomy. But he had told me nothing about his heart.

I tried to put my ear closer to the source of the sound. It kept saying, "Lub" skip "a-dub," in its slow and faltering way.

What if he died tonight? I thought about how tragic a figure I would be, a widow of an eight-day marriage. It happened sometimes. Well, we had had a perfect eight days—except for those few hours by Victoria Falls, I admitted to myself.

"Lub" skip "a-dub." If this heart decided it was too much trouble to do the next "lub," and just stopped, who would I run to tell? There certainly wouldn't be any paramedics nearby, or an ambulance. Maybe even the tall man in the black overcoat would have blown out his lantern and gone off to his bed somewhere. How would I find him in this frozen black atmosphere? And would I have to explain after all, in the end, why the deceased was Mr. Ackerman, not Mr. Collinson? There would have to be telegrams sent home, and what would I do with the body? Bury him here, that's for sure. Explorer Rhodes had his grave here in the Matopos, so there was precedent.

Suddenly I was angry at my thoughts. I wouldn't let him die! I had come too far for such an ending. Maybe it was better not to listen. After all, I didn't really know what his heart sounded like in broad daylight. Maybe in this cold he was just flirting with hibernation, not death. I moved my ear away from his chest and nestled into the hollow of his shoulder.

109

Oh, the dazzling daylight of the next morning! Still frosty cold, but what a landscape! The tall brown grass and the forests of Wankie Game Park had done nothing to prepare us for this fairyland, a giant's playground of rocks and boulders. Our hut was dwarfed by a tall wall of rock, and across the flowered yard was a tumbled rock heap, the rocks being more the size of our Dodge Dart than what you'd ordinarily expect in a rock garden. Off in the distance hills were strewn with odd-shaped boulders or bare stone masses. In many places the rocks sprouted out of the plain balanced in precarious columns, placed one upon the other and fitted together as if some giant child were playing "Blockhead" on the nursery floor. Indeed, my sense the night before of being on a different planet wasn't far off. Except that, by day, it looked like an inviting place to explore instead of an isolated, life-threatening, alien world.

For days, we hiked until we were tired, then drove around the park to observe the wildlife. Strings of dainty gazelles tried to outdo each other at leaping the highest across the dirt track in front of our car. At our approach, warthogs would toss hairy manes over their piggy little shoulders, stick tufted tails straight up in the air like spears held aloft, and trot away with snarls on their tusked mouths. The zebras were fat and a sparkling black and white, so placid that you would expect to find them in miniature in a nursery toy box, or full-size on a merry-go-round. We caught a few giraffes necking and agreed that it was the perfect pastime for giraffes.

One afternoon we found a trail to a prehistoric cave. It led over the hills and rocks a long way, a welcome exercise to warm our bodies, since the harsh cold persisted. (On our trip into Bulawayo for picnic supplies the first morning we had learned that there was a record-breaking low of 21 degrees Fahrenheit the night we were freezing in our unheated hut.)

Suddenly Robby, who was ahead, froze in his tracks. "A viper," he whispered. Around the other side of the sun warmed rock, exactly where one would naturally choose a handhold to help support the way down the wall where the path wound, lay coiled a thin dark serpent. No doubt he was enjoying the warmth of the sun as much as we were, but to me he was the embodied threat of all the poisonous snakes in Africa. (People said, "You're going to Africa? Aren't you afraid of snakes? Those black mambas are deadly, and the green ones too. And a spitting cobra never misses. Be sure to take a good snakebite kit along wherever you go.")

Robby edged a little closer, and I resisted an urge to pull him back. After all, he had survived two years in Africa, and his heart was still beating, no thanks to me. I whispered, "Snakebite kit, where are you when we need you most?"

Robby answered, under his breath, "Back in Lubumbashi in the refrigerator, of course, where antivenom must be stored."

Well, so much for a snakebite kit. We'd just concentrate on avoiding an encounter with the snake.

"A boomslang, maybe?" Robby said, with interest. As he leaned over the rock, a dislodged pebble rattled down around the snake, who slowly uncoiled and streamed away under the large rock we were peeping over.

"Come on, he's gone," Robby said, and slipped over the rock and on down the path. I followed quickly, before I could imagine the snake recoiling into striking position under the rock. If Robby went on, I wasn't going to bide my time around a snake den. I had followed him to Africa, and I could go past snakes to an old cave if that's where he was going.

That night we were again hungrier than the contents of our picnic basket would accommodate. At noon we had tried to heat up a tinned steak-and-kidney pie, but lacking the right kind of can opener as well as the oven in which to bake it properly, the meal was a definite failure.

"Why don't we go back into town and find a restaurant," Robby suggested, and I was certainly willing.

The brightly lit streets of Bulawayo were only an hour away from our camp, but the warm family-style restaurant already seemed like another world. The waitress was poised with her pencil to take our orders, but when Robby greeted her and began to order, she gave a little shriek.

"Oh, you're Americans! Congratulations! It's so exciting, what you've done!"

She waved toward a waiter who was passing by. "They're Americans! Isn't that marvelous!"

"May I shake your hand?" The man came over and smiled as if he couldn't believe his eyes as he took both of our surprised hands. "It's just fantastic. Congratulations! I really did not think it could be done!"

By now I had dropped the menu and could only stare.

"Why, thank you," I managed to stammer. People got married every day. Why should it be so remarkable in our case? True, they wouldn't get many honeymooners from the States here in Bulawayo. But how did they know? Was there stray rice in our hair, or did the simple gold band Robby had bought me in Kitwe, Zambia, look shiny and unaccustomed on my fourth finger?

But Robby's face was alight. "Susan, what day is this? The date, I mean. July the what?"

"It would be the twenty-first, I guess," I said hesitantly. "We've been married for nine whole days, and I didn't think it was that obvious anymore."

The waitress tripped back on excited feet. "Forgive me—now what were you ordering? I was just so excited. It was just marvelous on the telly this afternoon. I was late for work and didn't even care! You said fish-on-a-plank for two?"

"Yes," said Robby, "and do you happen to have a newspaper? We've been on the road and have missed all the details."

Now I was totally mystified. He had missed the details? I thought he was one of the main participants in the event.

She was back in a moment, waving the newspaper. I could see the bold black headlines and then at last everything made sense.

"MAN WALKS ON MOON!" And there was the picture of Neil Armstrong putting his left foot down on the gray lunar surface. There was yesterday's date, July 20, 1969. But of course, the moon walk! In my preoccupation with travel and wedding plans, I hadn't been paying any attention to current events.

Robby was beaming, and others came by the table to discuss the "giant leap for mankind" that Neil Armstrong had performed. On the verge of blushing, I tried to remember if I had made any reply that revealed my assumption that people were congratulating us on our marriage. I satisfied myself that I had been proper and relaxed to enjoy that hot, savory meal and the camaraderie in the restaurant that night.

Even out on the street, people recognized us as

Americans and stopped to heap praise on our country. For the moment, no one was mentioning the war in Vietnam, the race riots in Detroit, the other marks across the face of our nation and its various people. We had walked on the moon.

"Y'know what?" I asked drowsily as we drove back to our camp through the night that was not nearly so cold as that first night, nor did it feel to me in the least like outer space, as it had before. Who was I to have talked of lunar landscapes, when that very day a man had been taking slow, weightless steps through real moon dust?

"What?" Robby answered.

"I'm glad our honeymoon began before the moon was conquered. The moon seems more romantic as an elusive light in the sky than as an object of scientific exploration."

"Still, it's kind of remarkable that our honeymoon and the moon's coincided," Robby argued.

"Well, I guess I could look at it this way: the heavens wanted to celebrate our marriage, and so the moon received its first interplanetary guests in aeons. I *guess* they were first, anyway," I mused.

"Don't be so sure," Robby interrupted. "You're in Africa, you know. I heard that one student at Mulungwishi was totally unmoved at the news of the Apollo flights. 'What's so great about going to the moon?' he said. 'My uncle has been there twice.'"

I laughed, but only a little. Yes, I was in Africa. It was easy to forget that, here in a place still so influenced by the British. We could enjoy fish-on-a-plank, newspapers, a smooth-running car, national parks, the comforts and the accepted principles of our own Western world. But there was more to be learned about this continent. To the moon twice, huh? Would

I ever understand? Or would I be a stranger forever, looking in from the fringes?

11
Hurtling Toward Lusaka

The bridge over the breathtaking Zambezi gorge is certainly scenic enough a place to wait for a border crossing. The Victoria Falls Bridge was completed in 1905 as part of Explorer Cecil John Rhodes's vision of the "Cape to Cairo" railway plan. He had the bridge built across the gorge near the "Boiling Pot" so that the passengers could see, hear, and even feel the spray of the swirling waters. Since the spray of the crashing falls could fly upward over a thousand feet and be seen from a distance of ten miles, it wasn't hard to feel the kiss of the moisture borne on the wind. But, standing in line at Zambian customs and immigration, it wasn't easy to feel relaxed enough to really enjoy being suspended over such drama. We were anxious about getting out of Rhodesia, through the Zambian formalities, and on our way back to Lusaka for the night. Time wasn't the only constraint, however.

Robby explained: "You see, I got you a laissez-passer to leave the Congo and enter Zambia, and then return to the Congo again. The problem is, you were allowed only one entry into Zambia, and one return to the Congo. Your one return to the Congo is in order, but since you entered Rhodesia, and must re-enter Zambia in order to get back to the Congo, that makes two entries into Zambia."

"How could that possibly matter?" I asked.

"You'd lose your *visa d'etablissement* that I worked so hard to get you for being a temporary legal resident of the Congo. And that would mean that you couldn't stay here with me."

So it was serious. "Well, what can we do?" At this point I couldn't see going back to writing love letters.

"We can't pretend we've never been in Rhodesia," Robby said. "Unless—"

I broke in. "I didn't want to go to Rhodesia badly enough to get sent home for it. Or put in jail. Or detained at the border." I remembered with a shudder the little hut at the Congolese border and the arrogant official who did his best to find any irregularity.

Robby paid no attention to me and continued with his train of thought. ". . . unless I could try to get them to stamp your entry on a different piece of paper, on the back of the passport, or something. I'll try something." He tried to act nonchalant, but he wore that strained, preoccupied look that I hadn't seen since the day before our wedding. "Remember when we entered Rhodesia a few days ago, the agent was very helpful and stamped our entry on an attached piece of paper. Rhodesia is tied too closely with South Africa for the Congolese, and I just thought it would save trouble. Now that we're back in Zambia, let's hope things will work out just as well."

Surprisingly, the immigration agent agreed, when Robby had explained the situation, not to stamp the entry on the customary place on my passport, but to use the attached paper. I relaxed and felt calm again. Things were going so well. It had really been a perfect honeymoon. And soon we would be cozily installed in our first home. I had a tempting vision of myself kneeling in a brick courtyard, transplanting a crisp fern, while the smells of baking cinnamon rolls drifted out of the kitchen window, and Robby. . . .

"We hope you enjoy your stay in Zambia." The immigration agent was smiling up at us. There was a sudden "thunk-thunk," and with one motion he had stamped the two passports squarely in the middle of the page reserved for visas, and was handing them across the desk to us.

I stared at my stamped passport. "But—I thought you said you wouldn't stamp. . . ."

The man was genuinely dismayed. "Oh, I'm so sorry. Please excuse me. I stamp so many passports every day; it was just from force of habit."

Mumbling a rather glum forgiveness, we exchanged despondent glances, picked up the offending passports, and went on. Now, bold as brass, my passport sported its two entries into Zambia. Knowing how the Congolese agent searched with a fine-tooth comb for any real or imagined irregularities, I needed to prepare myself for the worst. I had plainly overstepped my limits as a temporary resident of Zaire.

"What will we do now?" I almost wailed. There seemed to be no way of disguising the bare facts.

"Well, we have a couple of days to think of something," Robby tried to reassure me, but he didn't sound very hopeful.

We reentered Livingstone, Zambia, on a rather glum note. Driving through the small town, we headed north to Lusaka.

"Stop!" I said suddenly. It was as if something were calling to me. "Remember that tourist shop we were in last week? There's something I can't get out of my mind."

"The tired old elephant with the one broken tusk?"
Robby remembered the bleached wood carving, too.
While a glossy, polished mahogany carving had no
charm for us, somehow in this particular work of art,
the artisan had expressed in an arresting way the
dusty wrinkled body, the majestic slow motion, and
the weariness of years of trampling the countryside
as this giant African beast. At the time we weren't
sure how our money for the trip would hold out, so
we hadn't bought anything, just looked and remembered. But the bread-and-cheese picnics and the
camp-cot rondavels had helped us stay within our
budget, and in two days we'd be back in Lubumbashi.
We could afford such a special wood carving as this.

Going back through town to find the curio shop, we
chose the old elephant lovingly out of a group of five
or six of the same style and had him carefully
wrapped. I was ready to go, but Robby kept going
back to another display case full of roughly hewn
black fetishes. Near-human figures they were, but
misshapen and sinister. He kept eyeing the ugliest
one. The squat body had a huge protruding stomach
and somehow it had three arms as well, one of them
connected strangely with the potbelly.

"You don't really like that, do you?" I said hopefully.

"It's interesting, isn't it?" he said with enthusiasm.

"It *is* very interesting to look at in a shop or museum, but I certainly wouldn't want such a spirit
around my house to look at every day." I tried to
speak firmly, but I had a sinking feeling.

"Well, something *that* ugly ought to keep evil spirits away, not invite them, right?" Robby's tone became decided. "No, I like the fellow, I really do. You
don't mind, do you?" he asked without looking at me

as he signaled to the salesperson which carving he wanted.

Well, I had my elephant tucked under my arm, and if he really wanted the ugly thing. . . .

As we left Livingstone behind, the afternoon sun on our left and sinking, I heaved a deep sigh of contentment. With a straight run before us and time for some cozy chats, here we were on the road together again. But before I could even begin to hum a bar of some relaxing love song, I sensed that something was not right. The wind was shrieking past my ventilator. I closed it, and still the impression of a gale ripping past was very strong. I leaned over to the glass and examined the sky. It was calm and cloudless, and barely a shiver was passing through the foliage of the trees we zipped past.

"Seems fast!" I turned to face Robby's set profile after a minute of taking stock.

"Sixty miles per hour," was his terse answer.

"Isn't that fast for a gravel road?" I ventured, with apologetic overtones in my voice meant to indicate that I really knew *nothing* about driving in Africa, but was just wondering.

"On a straight stretch, it's the way we drive here," he said. "And, besides, I figured that to arrive in Lusaka by eight or nine o'clock, I'll have to maintain that speed. It's three hundred miles, and there'll be slow zones through villages. To find a hotel and to prevent maybe being stranded in the dark somewhere, I'd rather get to Lusaka as soon as possible. There are bandits on these roads, people say. By the way, is your door locked?"

I guiltily pushed down the button. He was so unreasonably apprehensive about theft and security. I hoped he wasn't paranoid. My nonchalance about such things would certainly be a sore point in our marriage, the way things were going. I couldn't remember the song I was going to sing.

I looked out the window. How could sixty miles an hour feel so much like flying? Maybe I had already absorbed the slow African pace of life that made our rate of speed excessive by contrast. We were slowing down now for a village. Little boys leaped out at the car, shouting, opening and closing their fists in a fast motion to try to tell us that our lights were on. Robby let them enjoy the illusion of having been helpful, by flicking off the lights until he had passed them, and then turning the lights back on as a safety measure. When this happened in every village we passed, the process got to be a bit of a bore.

"Well, anyway, it keeps you awake," I commented after the first hour and the first twenty repeats of the shouting and the turning-off-and-on-of-lights process.

There was no answer. I looked again at Robby's profile. The chin was grim, and the eyes set like steel on the road before him. There wasn't the remotest possibility that he could yawn or blink tired eyes. I shouldn't have implied that he could.

Hurtling through another village, I pretended to stretch my arm and body a little and sneaked a surreptitious glance at the speedometer. The indicator rested on the center of the twenty-five-mile mark. How it could feel so much like hurtling at that speed, I had no idea, unless there was something about the languor of the sheep and goats along the roadside and people gathered to rest under mango trees that made us speed-demons by comparison.

According to the map we would enjoy a clear road for a while. The straight stretch was in sight, but at the town's last intersection, a man leaped out at us,

waving his arms. I expected the twenty-first obser-
vance of the light-flicking ritual, but instead, Robby
put on the brakes. Then I, too, noticed the uniform. A
policeman!

Robby rolled down his window and greeted him.
But the excited officer ignored the formalities. "Are
you aware of the speed limit?"

"Yes," Robby said. "Twenty-five miles an hour, sir."

The man didn't listen. "You were speeding down
this street at a dangerous rate, certainly not twenty-
five miles an hour. You Americans with big cars think
only of yourselves. There are children who walk home
from school along this street. Think of them!"

Robby was offended at the very idea of driving reck-
lessly. "Sir, I had my eye on the speedometer. It was
on exactly twenty-five miles per hour." I leaned over
and offered a supporting nod.

The policeman looked at him scornfully. "You were
speeding, and you were a menace to the highway."

There was nothing else to be said. Though he had
no instrument to measure speed, there was an air of
authority about the tall Zambian officer, and there
was nothing to offer but a sincere, if baffled, apology.
He softened then, and let us go on, cautioning us
with strict orders to drive within the law.

It was puzzling. It had always been a point of honor
with Robby to obey traffic laws exactly. Back in Virginia he wouldn't start the car until I was buckled
into my seat belt. (This had provoked rumors that we
were just friends instead of sweethearts, sitting so far
apart on the ample front seat of the green and white
1955 Chevrolet.) How could he be speeding today? I
had seen the speedometer for myself.

Now the atmosphere in the car became even grim-
mer. I attempted a few subjects of conversation, but

the driver's attention was riveted to the slippery gravel road. The way was straight and open again, and his
speed was back up to exactly sixty. His arms shook
with the vibrations that passed up through the steering as the tires split through the rough gravel. There
were few other vehicles on the road, thankfully, and I
thought it would be better if I could sleep a while,
but holding my eyes shut as we sped down the road
was an impossibility. Catastrophe seemed too likely
to be only just around the next corner, and I wanted
to meet it with my eyes open.

At one intersection, a shiny black British Jaguar
was idling at the road coming in from the right, waiting to join us on the road to the capital city.

Robby's shell cracked just the slightest. "What a
car!" he said admiringly. "Watch how quick he leaves
us in the dust!"

I waited to see the car nosing around us, not deign-
ing to turn my head to watch its progress. About ten
minutes later, it occurred to me that no Jaguar was
forthcoming.

At the same time, Robby said in a puzzled voice,
"Now what happened to that guy? I don't even see
him in the road behind us anymore. Must have been
something wrong with his Jag."

Somehow the time passed. The sun fell low and
ducked behind each tree on our left as we whipped
by. We had to be at least halfway to Lusaka, I was
sure, since it was near six o'clock. We seemed to be
approaching another town. From the outskirts, it appeared to be quite a big town. I could see high-rise
hotels and apartments in the distance. It looked
like—but couldn't possibly be—Lusaka.

"What town is this?" I asked Robby.

His face wore a strange look of disbelief invading

the fatigue and strain already mirrored there. He looked at his watch, at the speedometer, and ahead at the city, most undoubtedly Lusaka, glowing red-orange in the horizontal rays of the setting sun. "Lusaka," he said.

"But how can it be? It's three hundred miles, and we left Livingstone less than four hours ago."

"Then it couldn't be sixty; that's *eighty* miles an hour," Robby said incredulously. "What is wrong with this car? We worked for weeks, getting it in perfect shape. We spent *days* on just the wheels. We couldn't find thirteen-inch ones anywhere, so we had to install fifteen-inch rims, even though it meant cutting the studs off the brake drums and resetting them to match the holes. Then we could put fifteen-inch wheels on, and we were ready to roll."

"But—big wheels—don't they go faster? I mean, further on one turnaround."

"Oh, that's right." Robby was quiet for a moment, calculating. "The circumference of a fifteen-inch wheel would be about a third again that of a thirteen-inch wheel. With the speedometer set for the small wheels, I *was* doing eighty instead of sixty, and on that dangerous gravel road!"

"Now it makes sense," I muttered, inwardly begging forgiveness of the concerned Zambian policeman and everyone who had had to duck the gravel spurting from under our oversize tires.

Never did I feel a larger gulf between me and the African scene than I did at that moment, and in the next fifteen minutes, when we checked into Lusaka's Intercontinental Hotel. Exhausted, we welcomed the hot water, private bath, telephones, room service, and a double bed where two people could actually sleep together in spacious comfort.

Even after bathing and trying to rest a bit, it was almost impossible to eat our dinner at ten o'clock that night. The bamboo-and-jungle decor of the Snack Shop did nothing to stop that fork from shaking when Robby tried to eat an omelet. Even sleep was long in coming.

"Look at you," I said. "If we'd have gone by my intuition, we'd have slowed down no matter what that speedometer said."

He managed a sheepish grin. "Well, you just need to learn to be more forceful when you're right and I'm wrong."

"That's easy to say in retrospect!" I laughed, but at the same time, I filed the comment away for future reference.

12
Night of the Five Bandits

Something was terribly wrong. I sat up in complete darkness, trying to remember what bed I was in and at the same time make sense of an awful sound whose echoes were still tearing through my head. I couldn't manage either one and was only just beginning to remember whose inert sleeping body that was, pressed close to mine, when the agonized scream ripped through the black nothingness again. This time, along with the despairing scream, there came the slam of a screen door and then running feet—one pair. That was all. No voices, nothing more. The moment dissolved into the black night leaving no reverberations except in my whirling mind. Slowly, the memory of my surroundings began to settle in around me—the guest room and hospitality of Harold and Christine Wenger, the grounds of Chipembi Girls School, and the knowledge that we were in a compound of teachers' houses close together.

The panic I had felt at the Matopos imagining Robby's heart stopping washed back over me, and I knew that someone had died. I waited for the sound of people coming to help—voices, footsteps, doors, reassuring human noises. With all my senses straining for reassurance, there was only nothing. I might have been blind and deaf for all the good my efforts did.

Why weren't Christine and Harold getting up to do something? Was I the only one who had heard the screams? I wanted to awaken Robby, but it was so good to see him sleeping so deeply, after the sleepless night in the Lusaka Intercontinental. And the next day we would be going on. He needed that restful sleep. I waited for another scream.

The next minutes didn't go by like tidy little watch-tickings. In the nothingness the minutes seemed elastic and sticky, stretching into each other and pulling time both backward and forward so that it seemed not to be going anywhere at all.

Finally, I eased my tense body back under the blankets and tried to relax. Without some further input from the scene of crisis, my thoughts had nowhere to go. Perhaps I had dreamed the whole thing. I tried to think about something else, about the fun of being with Harold and Christine these last two days.

Christine Headings and I had brushed our teeth in the same bathroom every morning of our freshman and sophomore years at Eastern Mennonite College. And though one might think that an awkward occasion for talking, we managed very well. Harold Wenger was my double second cousin from Chesapeake, Virginia. The two of us claimed as great-grandfathers both Isaac D. Hertzler and Daniel P. Shenk.

I had been so pleased when Harold and Christine were married, and even more pleased when they came through MCC's Teachers Abroad Program to the same school my sister Connie and her husband, Jim Lehman, were teaching at in Chisamba, Zambia. Connie, Jim, and daughters Anne and Linda had returned to the States the year before, but having the Wengers there gave us an extra reason to take a fifty-mile jog out of our way and visit the place and people we had heard so much about. And, indeed, Chipembi Girls' School seemed a refreshing and familiar port in the sea of dust through which we rolled up to the Wengers' door—at a careful and moderate speed, of course.

What a warm feeling I had coming into their home that first evening! It wasn't just the cocoa and popcorn, the furious games of kangaroo Chinese checkers. It was that, for the first time, I felt affirmed in our marriage by friends and relatives, the reality that was lacking in our wedding ceremony for me because no one familiar was there.

But those screams—I was suddenly back to wondering. Could burglars have broken in and hurt someone? It seemed so unlikely a place for an armed robbery, this sleepy little school compound. Robby had been surprised just the night before to see that Harold ordinarily left his little Volkswagen unlocked, windows open, and the keys in the ignition. Of course Robby couldn't feel comfortable doing the same, but it certainly made us feel relaxed and secure, almost like we were still back in rural Virginia in the 50s.

As hard as I listened, nothing more came to me that night except the far-off sleepy crows of a rooster, and before I knew it, breakfast sounds were coming from the kitchen.

The Wengers didn't seem surprised about the scream I described at the breakfast table. "It's the couple next door," Harold explained. "She hates it here and wants to go back to England. He thinks they should finish out the year. So they fight about it. She probably just slammed out of the house and went to stay with a friend for the rest of the night."

It was too much for me to understand. I felt like a stranger here in Africa myself, but that would change, wouldn't it, during the course of the coming year? I had a swift vision of myself screaming at Robby that I wanted to go home, and him too weary of my scenes to even try to comfort me. It was a chilling thought, and I abandoned it quickly. Luckily, the conversation was getting interesting.

"Really, you ought to stay another night," Harold was saying. "It's Sunday, and we can go to early services and then we're free all day."

"I really should be back at the Social Center by day after tomorrow," Robby said regretfully. "We've been gone two whole weeks."

"But once we get back to Lubumbashi, there we'll be for the rest of the year," I reminded him. "No family, no old friends, no Chinese checkers kangaroo-style—and no popcorn, either! How long will it take us to drive back, if we get an early start tomorrow?"

Robby began to weaken. "We'll spend the night in Kitwe; then, if we leave early the next morning, we can be in Lubumbashi by noon. That's time enough to stick my nose in at the Social Center, I'd say."

The day was lovely, exploring the farm related to the school, taking back roads through the hills until they became footpaths, stuffing ourselves with good food, comparing "life-in-Africa" stories.

That last night we stayed up till midnight, reluctant to put an end to the tales we were exchanging. By this time we had reverted back to college days. Harold, Robby, and another teacher Ray Cope, each tried to top the stories of the other. Robby was going strong. There were his escapades in avoiding North Carolina policemen while he tore down Ku Klux Klan posters; there was the time he pretended to have been run over by his friend's car only to find that the worried driver was a complete stranger; there was the night he spent in a small-town jail because there was a law against sleeping on the Carolina beach in your car and he had spent his last forty-nine cents on a huge sack of animal crackers; then there was the time he fought a forest fire all night long and nearly got expelled from school because his blackened clothes were considered evidence that he had crawled through the coal cellar of a girls' dormitory and taken part in a panty raid. The others were doing their best to top these stories.

We went to bed in the wee small hours still laughing, full of a happy sense of well-being and fatigue. Let someone scream tonight, I thought, and I'll not even twitch an eyelid.

Morning came all too soon. On the morning of a trip, Robby gets up all business, because packing is his special, God-given vocation, and the order of the car must be perfect before he even thinks about breakfast. He took the suitcase and went out of the guest room. I was still dressing when he came back into the room rather abruptly and gave me a strange look.

"Can I see your extra set of car keys?" he asked in what was meant to be a normal tone of voice, but was shot through with slivers of tension.

"Of course, but why?"

He didn't answer, and I asked again as I rummaged in my purse. "Why? Can't you find yours?" I handed him my keys, totally mystified as I saw in his left hand his own set of keys.

Still not answering, he held the two sets of keys for a moment, looking me up and down as if I should be able to solve some mystery for him.

"You didn't give these to anybody, did you?" he asked, finally.

"Well, no, obviously, nobody but you," I spluttered. "What's the matter? Can't you unlock the car?"

He sighed. "I think I told too many college prank stories last night," he said with an edge of annoyance in his voice. "Somebody's trying to give me some of my own medicine."

"What's happened to the car?" My heart fell.

"I'm not sure," Robby answered. "Come here."

We walked out the back door, past the suitcase where it had been dropped at the bottom of the steps, and there was nothing. I don't know what I expected to find, but certainly a car in some condition. Harold's blue VW was sitting there as smugly as ever, keys dangling in the ignition, windows rolled down, but no big white Dodge Dart.

"We're a day late already, and we don't have time to play games," Robby muttered, but he had a funny look on his face as he examined the scuffed dirt around the place where the car had been parked. Maybe it wasn't a game. Maybe the infamous car was gone for real.

The surprise on Harold's face when he looked around for our car was so genuine that any idea of a "post-college" prank was abandoned in short order. "We'd better check around with the neighbors and see if they know anything," he said.

But news travels fast; the neighbors were already gathering. Peter Stead was a Scotsman who lived in the house my sister's family had lived in the year before. "I heard a car being pushed past my house," he said. "Then I heard it start up, out on the road, and roar off."

It appeared that nearly everyone on the compound

131

had heard suspicious noises the night before. They had shined their flashlights around their own property and, reassured, had gone back to sleep. One lady had even seen the shadowy figures pushing the car and, attributing it to some American foolishness, fixed herself a cup of tea and got lost in a detective story till she could get back to sleep.

"Has anybody called the police?" I wondered.

Robby and Harold exchanged knowing glances, and Robby made excuses for me. "She's new to Africa," he laughed. "The police, Susan, are more of a formality here than anything else. We'll notify them, of course, and they may have some leads, but it's a question of transportation and resources. It's the same in the Congo. I've had policemen there flag me down in my Volkswagen, hop in, and say, 'Follow that car!' They just don't have the vehicles and the fuel to pursue anyone. Then when we lose the guy we're chasing, they'll say that it was probably some thief from Zambia slipping through the border a back way. They always seem to enjoy the ride."

Harold laughed. "You wait and see. The policemen here will say it was Congolese bandits that slipped down over the border and took your car!"

The men went about organizing their own search. Harold had to go on and teach his classes, but he lent Robby his car. Robby seemed quite relaxed again, now that the worst had happened. I was surprised at his calm until I remembered how many times he had successfully recovered his stolen racing-striped car in Lubumbashi. This was familiar ground!

"They'll be near here somewhere," Robby said. "There was plenty of gas in the car, but what they do is, they park it somewhere out in the bush and strip the battery and other removable parts. Of course,

132

there's always the possibility that they went into hiding until things blow over and they can take the car somewhere to sell it. I could take your car, Harold, and see if I could track the tires in the dust. They were Goodyear tires."

"Of course. I was going to suggest the same thing," agreed Harold.

I looked around the yard with its useless traces of human footsteps and tire tread. Our suitcase was still sitting by the steps looking as if it had just missed a train. I felt a bit out of place myself, so I picked up the suitcase and walked back into the house. Detective work wasn't much in my line.

It struck me how light this suitcase was now compared with a few weeks before when it was weighed with a heavy hand at Patrick Henry Airport. And then something else struck me.

"Christine!" I groaned. "All of our dirty clothes from the whole two weeks were in our laundry bag in the back of the car. They're gone!"

"All your clothes?" she asked.

"Nearly everything. We didn't do any laundry at all on the trip, and thanks to the trousseau showers the EMC people and my Yoder aunts had for me, I had actually had enough underwear—nice, new, matching sets of underwear—blues and yellows and lacy beige—to last the whole two weeks. And most of my shirts and skirts and dresses were in there to be washed, too."

Christine was ready to take me shopping for cloth and start sewing some new clothes right then and there.

"Thanks, but who knows, Robby might get them back. Let's wait a bit and see. After all, it's just underwear. Now if they'd taken the afghan I was knitting, I'd really be upset." I looked around me for a moment. "Don't tell me—Christine, the afghan's gone, too!"

"There was an afghan in the car?" Christine tried to understand how this could be such a tragedy compared to all that lingerie.

I sighed. "It was really stupid, to take a knitting project on a honeymoon. I haven't knitted a single row, of course. But the afghan meant something special—it was a challenge, a very difficult Aran fisherman pattern, composed of long creamy strips of various widths and types of stitches. It was going to be beautiful. But sometimes I knit because I *need* to knit. It sorts out my mind; I feel centered somehow; and my thoughts get happy and creative and. . . ." I broke off and managed a little smile. "I wish I had those knitting needles right now." I kept thinking of more things that were gone. "The Samsonite flight bag Connie bought me—we picked it out together in Richmond; the tired old elephant carving—oh, well, give me something to do, Christine. It's not doing me any good to talk about what's gone."

Robby and another MCC volunteer Gale Maust had long since departed in search of the stolen vehicle, when about midmorning, billows of dust announced the approach of a vehicle from the direction of Lusaka. We watched as a Land Rover roared into the compound and squealed to an abrupt and smoking halt. The doors popped open, and Zambian policemen in crisp blue uniforms jumped out, poised as if to catch the car thieves red-handed.

Since there were no thieves to be seized on the spot, they stayed and speculated a while. The villains were, of course, armed Congolese bandits that had slipped over the border, they explained. Not that they had seen them yet, but their night's itinerary was plain enough. The little British station wagon languishing in the road near the school with two flat tires had been swiped in Lusaka when their first effort, a stolen Land Rover, ran out of gas before they got out of town. Someone in Lusaka had seen the thieves and said there were five of them.

At least that explained why they took the trouble to force open and hot-wire our Dodge when Harold's VW sat humbly unprotected with keys in the ignition. Five big men would fit into the Dodge better than into the Volkswagen. I was glad now that no one had awakened to challenge them.

The police went back to Lusaka to keep headquarters warm in case of any new information filtering through. That was the last any of us saw of the Zambian police.

Robby came home that afternoon, dusty and hot and without a single new clue. "I found a set of Goodyear tires, all right. They looked nice and new, just like ours. I tracked them for miles and miles. Pretty soon the road dwindled and led uphill. There were big ruts and almost impassable washouts, but I was sure I was on the right track, because it would be just the place to hide a stolen car. I came into a village, and there were the Goodyear tires—on an ox cart halted in the shade of a giant mango tree."

So much for the ground search. That evening, a neighboring British rancher, trying to be helpful, came over with a new idea.

"I'll be glad to take you up in my small airplane tomorrow morning. We can buzz the area in case the car is hidden nearby somewhere off the road."

Robby was delighted. Had he forgotten how he felt in a plane, particularly in small acrobatic aircraft?

If he had, his memory was refreshed early the next morning. After an hour or two of swooping, buzzing, and looping around and over every clump of trees for many square miles, Robby was deposited back at the Wenger's house, gray as a ghost. There hadn't been a single gleam of white metal in the whole area, but the pilot had certainly had a chance to practice all his fancy climbs and dives.

"I never realized how hard it is to vomit with your eyes open," Robby said weakly. "I had to keep looking for that car with every roller-coaster dive he made." He stayed in bed for the rest of the day, too sick even for a game of Chinese checkers.

The morning of the third day I began to wonder how long this was going to take. Even good friends' hospitality could be stretched to the limit, and at some point we might have to just acknowledge that the car was gone with no clues. Robby was just deciding if his legs were seaworthy after twenty-four hours of rest when he was called to the school's telephone. It was the Zambian police, who reeled off some rather vague directions to where our car had been seen, unfortunately in a smashed-up condition. So, it was found at last! Forgetting yesterday's nausea, Robby drove off with chains and tools northward toward Kabwe, along the highway that bisects the country—and leads, naturally, to the Congo!

Seven hours and three hundred fruitless miles later, Robby drove back into the compound. To his surprise, the car which had eluded his search was standing in the Wenger's yard, barely recognizable, but there. Neighbor Peter Stead was there, too.

"I was the one who called the police this morning and reported that I had found the car," he explained to Robby, who was relieved to see the lost found, but totally mystified. "I was driving into Lusaka by a back road and there it was, smashed and abandoned only about twenty miles away from here. It was straddling a nine-foot drainage ditch where it must have sailed off the road and smashed into the far side of the gully. I was on my way to an appointment, so I just telephoned the police when I got into town. Didn't they call you?"

Robby looked chagrined. "Yes, they called me, but they sent me off in the opposite direction."

"Well, anyway, here she is. On my way back from town this afternoon, I saw the car was still there, so I towed her on in behind my car."

Thanking Peter, Robby lost no time in looking the car over. It was totaled. By *any* standards, the car was totaled. I had a sick feeling in the pit of my stomach imagining the impact the men inside had sustained when the driver lost control. I wondered what the five alleged "Congolese bandits" looked like now—the one who broke the steering wheel on impact, the one who left blood and hair in the shattered safety glass of the windshield, the ones in the backseat whose impact tore both back and front seats from their mounting and who left blood both inside and outside of the car. There was no further trace of the thieves, who, it appeared, had already paid for the night's joyride.

The surprise accident must have prevented the bandits from taking everything from the trunk of the car, but someone was in good-enough shape to select the best of the clothes from the laundry bag. Choosing only half of every matching set of underwear, this person obviously preferred a rainbow effect. The half-finished afghan and the lovely flight bag were gone, as were my sunglasses, all the tools, the gas burner, the carvings, and the picnic items. They had obviously breakfasted on the stale remains of days of picnicking, because there was nothing in the basket except a tattered piece of pasteboard.

"The cake!" Robby said with regret. "They ate that last piece of wedding cake I was saving for an emergency."

"They deserved each other," I couldn't help saying, relieved that the fossilized pastry had reached its final resting place. "But I do hate to lose that old elephant," I added wistfully. "He meant something to me, the Africa I hope to know better."

"Wait! It may be here. This feels like a wood carving." Robby unwrapped paper from something he dragged out of the depths of the trunk. Out of the parcel emerged the hideous head and deformed arms of the carving Robby had found so appealing in the Livingstone curio shop. "Look!" he said delightedly. "Here's a survivor! The robbers didn't dare touch him!"

I thought of the gentle, tired lines of the elephant, the wrinkled grace of his carriage, and then looked again at the rough ugly fetish. "What do I want with a fetish that protects only itself?" I said. "I'd rather have my elephant, not to mention my flight bag and my new clothes."

But Robby's thoughts turned back to the condition of the car itself. He pointed out every detail to me. "Here, the fire wall is split across from one side to the other. The transmission hump has those three bulges where the car was compacted in the crash. The radiator and all the metal in front is completely smashed. The front suspension is bent in every conceivable direction. The cast-iron pulleys on the engine are cracked into pieces. None of the doors will open. It's totaled."

I felt tired and headachey. Was this wreck what we had been looking for all this time? And what now that we had it?

"Well, how do you and I get back to Lubumbashi, then? Are there trains?"

He looked at me as though I were an ignorant four-year-old. "What do you mean, trains? We'll drive the car back!"

"But I thought you said it was totaled," I said, feeling confused.

"Well, it is," he answered.

"I thought totaled meant . . . well, finished," I said, trying not to sound apologetic.

He put his arms around me. "Honey, you've been putting up with a lot. I don't know a single other girl who would have come out here like this and married me and been spunky enough to take everything that's happened."

I wasn't sure whether that was a compliment or not, but I did start to feel a little better, encircled in his arms. He went on. "Here nothing is ever totally totaled. Gale Maust and I will get busy on this wreck, and in a few days you'll have a ride back to Lubumbashi that may not be luxurious, but it will certainly be a novel experience."

Four days later, we were on the road again, dust rolling up behind the car as we waved good-bye to the Wengers, and our spirits were high. It was actually running, this heap of twisted metal! People all along the way stepped out to the road to laugh and to let us know that our light was on. I say light, because, in place of the two smashed headlights, one lamp was mounted high on the front of the car, controlled by a manual toggle switch temporarily mounted on the dashboard. Robby obligingly reached down to flick the switch at the clamor of each group of roadside spectators.

I giggled. There was no way to see through my side of the windshield, shattered as it was, and with the wide gray duct tape spread across the crackled mess. The steering wheel had saved Robby's side, but I was perfectly at ease, not being able to see ahead. After all, our speed was now about half that of our Lusaka trip, and no longer was I convinced that disaster lay just around the bend. Disaster had already come and gone!

An approaching vehicle had a view of front tires angling off from each other at an improbable slant. The impact had splayed them out, and even the hammers Gale and Robby had used on the suspension parts had only brought them into an approximation of uprightness. The front fenders, the bumper, and grillwork were conspicuous in their absence, riding in state in the trunk. A square of the crumpled front had been cut out with a hacksaw, the ruined radiator replaced with a junked Toyota radiator salvaged at the local "car-breaker's," the English term for a junkyard. A length of garden hose made the connection to the motor, which in itself was not damaged, but the cast-iron pulleys which supported it had to be welded and welded until they somehow stuck together in spite of the fact that cast-iron isn't a metal that can be welded.

And, now, amazingly, the contraption was purring along the highway, attracting smiles of incredulity. I felt just a bit like the White Queen in *Through the Looking Glass*. When we were suspicious of impending trouble—theft, accident, breakdown—we were tense and uncomfortable, like the White Queen screaming because her shawl pin was going to fly open and prick her finger. When it did, Alice braced herself for even more horrendous screams, but instead, the Queen smiled happily. She had done her lamenting in advance. We were carefree and relaxed all the way up through Zambia, as our junk heap plowed along the road, evoking grins of good-natured ridicule all the way.

As we traveled along, I idly scanned the roadside for someone with a knitted strip of pale gold afghan wrapped around her head against the morning chill. For the remaining months of my year in Africa, looking for my afghan was to pleasantly fill many monotonous hours of travel or waiting in city crowds.

Our lighthearted mood lasted all the way to the frontier between Zambia and the Congo. As we approached the border, I remembered that we were supposed to be concerned about something—what was it? Oh, yes, losing my resident's visa because I had illegally exited and reentered Zambia in my absence from the Congo. Somehow, in our high spirits, neither of us could feel very nervous.

We drew up to the red and white pole that lay across the road just behind a smoking busload of Zambian travelers piled high with bags. Red dust swirled around our wreckage as it floated to a stop. The two immigration officials left the queue of Zambians and came out, delighted, to survey the damage. They clucked and "hmmmed" and asked questions. In their opinion, we were not surprised to hear, all the evidence pointed to a band of Zambian bandits, always out to get a car with honest Congolese license plates.

Either his stamping hand was weary after processing that busload, or our misfortune so pleased and gratified him that he had no urge to hassle us, but in any event, the officer never even opened my passport. Robby's was duly stamped and commented upon, but the man simply handed mine back along with Robby's. So I was no longer a person in my own right, but a piece of property—just so much baggage? Robby threw me a mischievous glance as he quickly tucked the passports away in his briefcase. Well, this was clearly not the time to campaign for my equal rights as a female American citizen. Saying anything at this point could mean an overnight wait on the dirt floor of the immigration office. We cut and ran.

We had sent a telegram ahead of us, of course, so none of the Methodist missionaries seemed surprised that we were home a week later than expected. They were mildly amazed at the condition of the car, however, and Robby enjoyed himself immensely telling and retelling the story of the theft and recovery of the ill-fated Dodge Dart.

As for the demolished car itself, we would never drive it again. Alex, the Pakistani mechanic who had helped get it running before the honeymoon, was delighted to buy such a luxury vehicle and lovingly rebuild it part by part. Long after the kinks had been pulled out of its chassis, and the body had been restored to a wrinkle-free gloss and painted a sophisticated green, Alex proudly drove around to all the night spots of Lubumbashi with the original shattered windshield still held together by the gray duct tape that had blocked my view all the way home from Chipembi Girl's School.

It was one day in August that Mary Ruth came by waving a garbled telegram. "News from the Ackermans! Says that your car has been stolen and that you won't be home for a few more days. Thanks for letting us know!"

13
Mistress of Maniema

It was midnight; I left Robby sorting letters in the study and walked out into the moonlit courtyard. Where did he get this burst of energy when I felt like collapsing into bed? I was exhausted with moving day, but not too exhausted to enjoy the slight breeze and the feel of the sun-warmed patio bricks under my feet. And the silence.

All afternoon, as we moved the final load of assorted mission belongings and our clothes to the Booth House here at 1431 Avenue Maniema, the drums beat next door. As we worked in the seasonal heat to put things away and to create a home out of an expanse of stone, stucco, and tile, those drums beat, and the singing grew louder and more furious.

Now they were silent. Now just the wide flat spiders on the bedroom wall, the dimness of the 40-watt bulb in the large, black-tiled bathroom, and the fact that my facecloth had been used as a cleaning rag remained to take the tiniest edge off my happiness.

I had not been eager to leave the Vanhee's honeymoon cottage and Leonard's light hand in the kitchen. But Bob and Lieve were about to return from vacation in Belgium, and it was time to find our own home. As it happened, the only mission residence that was available was this one. An impressive white stucco and natural stone edifice, the house had been built by Methodist Bishop Booth as his retirement home, a man who had given his years in the Congo and chose to die there. I was awed that such a house—67 feet wide and 53 feet deep—was to be our first home. With all that square-footage, however, it was still a one-bedroom house, built around a grassy courtyard, with a book-lined study, a sunlit corner office, and a large living room. At the time the home was built, the popular decorating colors were apparently black and turquoise. All the tile floors were black, and almost every wall a heavy turquoise. This presented quite a decorating challenge to a young couple with no money to spend on draperies and artwork, and very few earthly possessions to scatter around to soften the effect.

All afternoon I had felt almost homesick for the cozy cottage with its Belgian hemstitched cloths, its copper kettles and plaques glowing in the sun, its riot of flowers of every description tumbling over the entrance, its three tiny rooms. But tonight, breathing in the soft, gardenia-scented air, I was ready to tuck that lovely six weeks into our life's album as I had the wedding and the honeymoon. Tonight the stars above me, framed by the four walls, were deep and rich; they seemed happy to sparkle down on us, the ultimate in home decorating and ours for free.

Robby was still sleeping off his energy spurt of the wee small hours when I ventured eagerly into the kitchen. All the honeymoon breakfasts and Léonard's tomato omelets at the Vanhee's house didn't count. This would be Robby and me, lingering over our coffee and toast, savoring every moment of the gorgeous morning hour alone. I looked around the black-tiled kitchen. There was an electric range with two burners working, a refrigerator, a double sink with a window overlooking the courtyard, and a small table covered with oilcloth.

Scrambled eggs would be nice, I thought, remembering the half-dozen eggs in the otherwise empty refrigerator. And easy, too. Unless . . . unless there was something I didn't know about making really delicious scrambled eggs. Well, that's what this Betty Crocker book was for. Let's see. . . . "Eggs, scrambled, p. 257." Wait a second. Did I want creamy eggs? Not really; that sounded a bit nauseating for the first thing in the morning. Garnishes for? I checked out page 24. Julienne ham, pineapple marmalade, or sautéed mushrooms? Out of the question. Quick scrambled eggs? The urgency was lacking with the other breakfaster still in bed. Topped with smoked turkey? With cheese? With dried beef or ham? With herbs? With mushrooms? And here on page 257 were photographs: Pouring the beaten egg mixture into the moderately hot skillet, and gently and evenly lifting cooked portions with spatula to keep them moist and glossy. My stomach turned at the excessive glossiness, and I slammed the book shut.

It was then that I heard the discreet knock. At the kitchen door stood a neatly dressed man, small and straight, his sport jacket covering a fresh white shirt. It must be Kawanga Pascal, the man who was to come each day from seven to two and do housework, laundry, or cooking for us. I looked wildly down at the cookbook in my hand and felt guilty and inferior, a holdover from the days of Léonard, even though the man in front of me didn't look one bit threatening.

As soon as we had properly greeted each other, I made out a list of necessities for Pascal to get at the market. That would get him out of the kitchen until our breakfast was safely over. As I wrote, he watched closely and repeated several times after me: tomatoes, lettuce, onions, carrots, pineapple. Then he took his bicycle and a market basket and was on his way.

I heard the bathroom door close and knew that our conversation had awakened Robby at last. In a panic, I grabbed four eggs, cracked them into a skillet, and dumped in a dollop of the powdered milk I had mixed up the night before. A fork would have to do in the absence of a proper spatula, and I swirled it madly to keep the mixture from sticking to the battered pan. The results were decidedly not glossy, but I needn't have worried.

Robby's eyes looked puffy, and he seemed to stare in the direction of a particular spot on the turquoise dining room wall as he took his seat in the dining room.

"Tea or coffee?" I asked brightly. After the exertions of the early morning, all my adrenaline was flowing. The table looked as lovely as a fresh-cut green-and-red poinsettia on a black-and-white African print cloth could make it.

Robby looked pained. "Is there milk? How about half a glass of that?"

I poured his milk while he eyed the little dry mound of eggs on his plate.

"And here's the fresh toast and jam and butter," I said, passing the wooden platter that was heaped high. He took it politely, almost appreciatively, and set it back down on the tablecloth without taking any.

I reached for a piece of the toast, but the fun had gone out of buttering it. Robby, with a supreme effort, lifted a fork and began to move lumps of scrambled egg from the plate to his mouth. He was doing it just

146

for me. What our honeymoon breakfasts had hinted at was now very plain. There were to be no bright, cozy breakfasts. My lifelong dream of married bliss began to crumble and slip under the bright table. Ahead stretched a lifetime of unpleasant morning hours. No wonder he preferred to sleep until the last minute in the morning, while I wanted to get up and wrest each glowing moment from the freshness of the morning. Why had I married someone so different from me?

My mind drifted back three years. It was obvious that we were different from the very first evening we spent together. Exchanging dreams before the spitting fireplace at Chowning's of Williamsburg, I learned that Robby would be leaving for boot camp in just a matter of days. Dropping out of school after his sophomore year at Campbell College was an invitation to be drafted in this the height of President Johnson's military buildup in Vietnam, something Robby regretted but felt was necessary.

Being brought up in a "peace church" certainly influenced my emotional reaction to the idea of any military involvement, but my ethical stance was shared by lots of other Americans in those days, and I wondered how Robby could see it so differently. It was impossible to imagine this gentle, blue-eyed person I had just met in combat with any Vietnamese, whether villagers or villains. We were worlds apart, and he would go out of my life just as abruptly as he had popped into it. But, meanwhile, it was so pleasant to be together—and, as long as we both knew it was only for a few days. . . .

There were long walks, long talks, surprise boxes of candy. After his surveyor's work Robby would drop by the schoolhouse, where I'd be preparing my lessons

147

for the next school day. The fact that we were not involved with each other was so evident that I wasn't even invited to the farewell party his parents threw for him.

But one night after dark, there was a loud knock at my front door. Breathless from a mile's bike ride at top speed, he told me the news. He wasn't going to boot camp. He was staying here. To this day he has no idea what the rash was that had appeared on his neck and chest the day he had his physical exam for the army. But that rash, coming for the occasion and then vanishing never to return, accomplished the impossible. Demoted to 1-Y status, Robby was considered a danger to the health of the other soldiers, and his orders to report for boot camp were canceled with only five days to spare.

To me the turnaround was nothing short of a miracle. He was not going out of my life; in fact he seemed divinely destined to keep going my way. Since he was in the mood to see the world, I casually mentioned the Pax program of the Mennonite churches—the concept of approaching the rest of the world from the standpoint of a servant, a helper, a learner.

I blinked and found myself at the Lubumbashi breakfast table again, watching Robby put his fork carefully across the top of his plate, a few remnants of the eggs gathered neatly to one side. Well, the rest was history, and here we were together. What was so wonderful about crunching toast simultaneously? I poured coffee into a brown mug. It smelled good. He didn't know what he was missing, but why should I pout about it? Twenty years from now he might be the biggest breakfast-eater in the world. Surprises seemed to be the prime ingredient of our relationship.

Robby stood up, pushed his chair under the table, and came around to where I was sitting. He put his arms around me. "Thanks for fixing my breakfast, Susan. Sorry my appetite isn't better in the morning."

"Mine makes up for it," I said. "We're just different, that's all!" I shrugged, surprised to know it really didn't matter to me any more.

"We're different, all right, and I really like it that way," he whispered in my ear.

"Careful! I hear Pascal coming through the kitchen," I giggled as I jumped up out of his embrace. There were other ways to enjoy each other than to eat breakfast together, I thought, turning back for a quick kiss.

Out in the kitchen, I inspected Pascal's purchases. He had selected only the very best. Here were the onions, the pineapple exuding its perfect fragrance, the tomatoes, the fluffy buttery-looking lettuce. But what were these thick green stalks? I sniffed. Onions? The biggest green onions I ever saw. I guess they would be all right in a salad. But where were the carrots?

I took the list from the market basket and glanced at it. Pascal, watching me closely, repeated, *"Tomates, salade, oignons, ananas, poireaux."* He wasn't even looking at the paper.

"Poireaux?" I repeated, puzzled.

Pascal patted the fat green oniony vegetable. *"Poireaux."*

"Is it for a salad?" I asked, surprised.

"Oh, no. You cook it as a vegetable. It's especially nice in a white sauce," answered Pascal.

Ah, so this must be the famous leek of French renown! But why had he chosen *poireaux* when I had written *carottes*?" Ignoring the paper, he turned and began washing the vegetables. Suddenly my thoughtlessness dawned on me. I had given a written list to a man who could not read. *Poireaux* and *carottes* were near enough alike in French pronunciation that the mistake was logical.

"Pascal, maybe you could cook these leeks for lunch. And I want to be sure to watch how you do it, all right?" I asked, suddenly feeling as if this person was my friend for life, someone I would defend to the end.

And so it was. Gone was the sense of being an intruder in my own kitchen! Gone was the lack of ease at the idea of having a "servant." For the remaining time we were to live in Lubumbashi, Pascal was to be one of our closest friends. I think he found this couple of newlyweds an endless source of amusement. He chuckled to himself as he watched Robby bury a hose in the courtyard to make a fountain in the rocks. He liked asking me about my home, family, and native land. "Is the United States a big city?" he asked one day.

On days to come he would introduce me to the adventure of the central open-air market. The market was so alive. Nothing drab or utilitarian about the bright wrap dresses of the vegetable-sellers, or the brilliant headscarves rising high above intricate hairdos. Tomatoes, redder than any I'd ever seen, were arranged on a tripod of three, then stacked, one on one, as high as gravity would allow. Carrots, cabbages, parsley, folded lettuces; onions and potatoes by the kilogram, weighed on a balance with iron weights. These stands were just at the entrance, with an eye to attracting the European trade.

More interesting to the fly population and more novel to my Western eye were the tables to the back of the market, where darkened red meat and fish lent their odors to the warm air, where chickens flopped or lay passively in the dust, feet bound by vines, and where children bought something white and sour-smelling wrapped in green leaves and steamed over a pot. I wanted to feel the softness of the white powder piled high in this woman's basin—what was it? Or ask my mother—the expert on wild greens—how best to cook the perky bunches of red-stemmed leaves, still soaking their roots in a tub of water. Would that small dark bean-like seed make good baked beans? Another time I would find out, I thought, holding my fishnet bag of safe little carrots and a familiar brown onion close to my side and making my way out of the market. The good-natured cries of the women I hadn't bought from trailed after me, and I clutched my bag tighter to keep more aggressive vendors from stuffing bananas right into it.

A few days later, Robby came home from the office with something on his mind. "Let's drive out into the *cité*," he said. "I've been wanting to see the new house Pascal is building, since I've agreed to help him finance the tin for the roof."

Pascal lived in Commune Ruashi, commuting to work by bicycle. The word *commune* simply meant a political division, and the word *cité* signified an area with typical African housing and looking less like a European city than the main part of Lubumbashi. It was not a shantytown; though many houses were built of mud brick and thatched roof, others were masonry and sported more durable tin roofing.

Garden plots, flowers, and palm trees were crowded into any available space; families gathered around cooking pots on mats; little boys teased their sisters and rolled their homemade cars through the ruts made by the occasional taxi or truck. A young man laid out packets of cigarettes, matches, candles, and dry white cookies alongside tiny tins of tomato paste and assorted candies on a small table under the generous spread of a mango tree. On the other side of the trunk, two wrinkled grandmothers dipped sizzling doughnut holes out of bubbling oil and left their fragrance to tempt passersby to buy a grease-soaked newspaper cone of them. In a small shelter to one side I could see an artisan bent over a turning wheel, polishing with painstaking care some bits of green malachite for jewelry.

We drove slowly along, following the ruts, until the road came up against a tight hedge with only a small path penetrating it.

"Pascal's house isn't far away," said Robby, "but it looks like we'll need to leave the car and walk the rest of the way."

As I turned to open the car door, already a tangle of children pressed against it, shouting *"Muzungu! Muzungu!"* Feeling very much like the foreign stranger they were labeling me, I tried to make my way through the crowd and down the path. My plain knee-length skirt and white blouse suddenly looked strange even to me, and the pale arms and legs pushing their way through the tangle of dusty brown and flashing ebony limbs even stranger. I couldn't see my own hair, tumbling shiny and smooth and brown to below my waist, but the children of the *cité* certainly noticed it. How novel such a slippery growth must have seemed to the little girl there whose hair, soft and woollike, made a firm nest in which to carry a big bar of soap, leaving her hands luxuriously free.

Ignoring Robby, the pack of children behind me began to chant, "Ma-ma! Ma-ma!" and, gathering force, came pushing and running behind me, reaching out their fingers for just one touch of the swinging hair.

"Ma-ma! Ma-ma!" There must have been fifty children now, laughing, singing, and chanting, pushing for the privilege of feeling that strange hair. I turned and waved. A roar of delight broke out.

"We're almost there," Robby reassured me through the din, as Pascal's brand-new tin roof shone like a beacon, promising protection behind a closed gate. But he was smiling to see me the Pied Piper of Commune Ruashi.

14
First Fever

I was rocking in a ship with rotten planks, suspended over greasy black waters. A mountain of
slimy, wormlike threads grew on the deck before my
eyes and the knowledge overwhelmed me that I must
untangle them all one at a time. I began to sob, fighting with the blanket on the narrow hotel bed. And
then suddenly I was awake, my heart pounding. Relief
that all was just a dream soon gave way to the real-
ization that I was sick, sick to the very core of my
body. Too dizzy to stand, I crept into the adjoining
bathroom, thankful that the second-rate Lusaka Hotel
had a private bath.

It was the end of September. Bishop Shungu and a
colleague needed to be driven to Lusaka, where they
could get a plane to a conference in Botswana. The
bishop and my husband had developed a mutual admiration over the previous years, and whenever Bishop Shungu needed to go any distance, he preferred to
have Robby drive the car. Since Lusaka was an eight-
hour drive, we needed to spend the night in Lusaka
before driving back the next day. Ironically, the flight
had been canceled, and the men would be returning
with us the next morning to Lubumbashi, having to
miss the meeting in Botswana.

In the bathroom, the fixtures seemed to float and

waver in the air as the pain and nausea wracked my body. Finally, I pulled myself back to the bed and lay down. I was too sick to wonder what was wrong. I was too sick to see any reason to awaken Robby; after all, he would need to have his sleep in order to do a good job of driving the next day. Once I reached out my hot hand to feel his cool, solid arm on the sheet, but he didn't move.

Later, I was aware of him leaning over me. "Are you okay, Susan?"

"No," was all I could whisper. I felt his touch on my forehead, my arms.

"We've got to get you to a doctor," I heard him say, and when I next knew anything, I was in the car, riding through early-morning Lusaka. "I think doctor's offices here are called surgeries," he was saying to himself. The car hesitated. "There's a sign that says Surgery but, oh, never mind. There's a sign on the same door pointing the other direction, and it says Butchery. I'd better keep looking. It's probably too early in the morning for these offices to be open, anyway."

Eventually we reached a hospital. An Indian woman gave me an injection and said something about malaria; and the next thing I knew we were all in the car on the way back to Lubumbashi. The bishop and his colleague made room for the front seat of the Peugeot station wagon to be placed in a reclining position, and I lay there, limp and wretched, for the whole day.

Once, at Broken Hill (Kabwe), Robby stopped for fuel. A rarity in our travels in Central Africa, there was actually an outhouse of sorts at some distance from the station. As Robby busied himself with fueling the car, I decided to make my way over to the little rest room. A few steps into the journey, however, I realized I was too weak, and I wasn't surprised to find myself suddenly face down in the powdery dust of the roadside. The earth felt restful to me, and I just lay there, content never to move again.

A hand on my shoulder. I was being gently shaken. Aware of the impressive bulk of the good Bishop Shungu kneeling beside me, I tried to see through a mist where his dark face was looking with concern into my own.

"Are you feeling better?" he said in English. "Are you feeling better now?"

He really seemed to want me to say I felt better, so I breathed a weak yes, and lay there unmoving in the dirt. Sick as I was, I could see how relieved Bishop Shungu was when suddenly Robby appeared, smelling of gasoline fumes, and helped me up.

So this was malaria. No wonder people who had it didn't care if they lived or died. I lay in the moving car in a stupor, opening my eyes occasionally to notice that the angle of the sun had changed as the day wore on. I have no memory of the border crossings. Only that at last I was lying in the cool sheets of our own bed in Lubumbashi. A mustached face appeared high above me, muttering something in broken English about parasites, typhoid fever, and malaria. I felt the sting of another quinine injection. Though it didn't seem remarkable to me at the time, some of the missionaries were amazed that Robby could actually find a doctor that would make a house call. In their twenty years of knowing Lubumbashi, they had never heard of such a thing. Dr. Karistianos, a Greek, had a dispensary not far from our home, and, as the year went on, we were to see quite a bit of each other!

How grateful I was that Pascal was there! Though the thought of food was a horror to me, it was reassuring to know that each day as I lay sick, Pascal was going to the market, cooking Robby's meals, and keeping things tidy. As I began to be able, he brought me a tea tray. In the evenings, Robby would bring me outside into the inner courtyard to enjoy the freshness of the tropical night air and to see how the ferns were growing in his little rock garden.

Sometimes he read aloud to me a chapter from Dinesen's *Out of Africa,* one of the volumes that had weighted my heavy briefcase last July. Listless as I was, I had little in common with Baroness Blixen and her adventures managing a plantation in East Africa. Still, the words fell gently and beautifully on my ear.

One evening, when I was still feeling weak, Robby prepared the corner office as a guest room. "There's a couple who needs a place to stay overnight; they're passing through on a quick Africa tour. Don't you worry about it; Pascal can take care of their meals and everything."

The Smiths were an older couple, come to represent their church's giving to missions here in Katanga. They came and went and did their souvenir shopping. Late that night, there came an urgent knock on our bedroom door.

"Robby, there's something horrid on the wall above my bed! Can you come and kill it?" Mrs. Smith couldn't suppress a shudder. "It's like a huge flat spider, as big as my hand."

Robby sauntered into the guest room, where both visitors were rigid with dread. High on the wall, he saw the normal household fixture, a pale brown spider, thin as a piece of cutout construction paper.

"Oh, *that* spider," he said.

"Yes, isn't it the most gruesome thing you've ever seen? I knew something like this would happen if we

157

came to Africa! Will it bite?" She clutched her robe around her.

Robby slowly shook his head, enjoying the drama. "You wouldn't really want me to kill that spider. He's there to protect you from other things. And he'll stay up there on the wall. In the two years that I've been here, I've never seen those spiders running around over the beds or on people. So don't worry."

The couple looked incredulous. He expected them to sleep in the same room with this sinister creature? He had to be joking.

"So you won't kill the spider," Mrs. Smith repeated, desperately.

"Of course not," Robby said firmly. "It wouldn't be in your best interest."

The next morning the Smiths looked a bit wan, as though their rest had not been unbroken. I was up for the first time in days and felt a bit wan myself, but glad to be alive. I walked out to the car to say good-bye to them and to Robby. He was to drive the Smiths over the border into Zambia, as well as to pick up some educational supplies there in Kitwe for the Methodist secondary schools on his return trip. I hugged Robby and whispered to him to hurry back, and the white Peugeot with its daisy painted on the back pulled through the gate. I swung back the wrought-iron gate, secured it, and walked slowly around the house.

I was glad to be in Lubumbashi. Glad to be alive. Glad to be able to walk without falling down. The new Doberman pup we called Friday came quietly beside me as we walked around the house in the early morning sunshine. The "thorns of Christ" were full of soft coral blossoms guarded by fierce, thick spines. The avocado tree was green and lush. Glossy fringed banana leaves unfurled in the little grove, and Friday ran to hide and play in the thicket of bamboo. I picked a rough green lemon to make a refreshing drink, and the fragrance stayed on my hand the rest of the day.

Reading, writing, resting, I began to count the hours. Four hours to Kitwe, four hours back to Lubumbashi, one or two hours to rest and do business in Kitwe. I should expect him around six o'clock.

Halfway through dinner preparations, I felt exhausted. It seemed strange to have the whole kitchen in a turmoil and the house silent. Did I really have a husband driving home through the perils of the African bush?

Dark fell. Friday paced the front rooms of the house, listening as I was for the sound of the car. The muffins were done. They would dry out in the oven. They would get cold and tasteless out in a basket. I picked a fragrant white gardenia and placed it on the table, on the blue and green linen tablecloth Robby had bought for me. Then Friday leaped up at the door with a high, sharp bark, and I, too, heard the sound of the car, stopping at the gate. In a few moments, I was in Robby's arms in the gardenia-soft darkness.

I needn't have worried about the dinner. Hot food made Robby's nose run, anyway. The cold muffins were just the way he liked them. Buttering his second, he started to laugh. "The funniest thing happened on the way back. You know I had a load of school equipment to pick up in Zambia, including a life-size plastic skeleton to be used in the science classes at Mulungwishi. The back of the station wagon was full, so, just for fun, I set the skeleton up as a passenger in the backseat. You know how the immigration control is quite some distance from the customs control as you cross the border into Zaire.

159

"Well, one of the agents—the one who always gives me a hard time—finally accepted the fact that he wasn't going to get any money from me, but he thought at least he could insist on getting a ride in my car from customs to immigration. He just opened the back door and slipped in, not waiting for an answer. I drove off, the fellow talking a blue streak, and we'd gone about a hundred yards, when he abruptly stopped in the middle of a sentence. There was silence from the backseat—total silence. We rode like this all the way to immigration control. As I slowed to stop, the passenger door opened, and the man was gone without so much as a thank you, or 'See you next time.' His 'grave' companion just sat there grinning white in the twilight. It was the best thing that's happened to me in a long time."

We laughed together in the gardenia-scented dining room, feeling the ridiculous exuberance of sharing a life full of surprises. I was especially grateful to have routed the malaria—hopefully forever. After all, I faithfully took that Daraprim pill each Sunday. Daraprim was a wonder drug to prevent malaria and I'd have to make doubly sure I took it strictly on schedule. I wasn't going to be sick like that again.

15
Back-door Morgan

The noon whistle sounded long and loud over the city of Lubumbashi. I walked into the dim coolness of Robby's office in the Centre Social Méthodiste and dropped my stack of English exercise books on his desk and then collapsed into his empty chair. How could four hours of teaching English to ninth- and tenth-graders totally drain me, mentally and physically? Thank goodness it was only two mornings a week, Tuesdays and Wednesdays. It felt like eighty hours instead of eight.

A cheerful face appeared in the door, topped with a round, white, close-fitting cap. It was Baba George, the administrative assistant at the social center. "Mama Lobby, Mama Lobby, *comment vas-tu* (how is it going)?"

I greeted him warmly. Now that I understood that Mama was the Swahili equivalent of *Mrs.*, it wasn't such a shock to be called that. Realizing that r's and l's were interchangeable to a Swahili speaker helped me make sense of the rest of my title—Mama Lobby.

Robby came out of the library, smiling. "It's full of kids in there," he said proudly. "I finally figured out how to get them into the library and over their fear of taking books off the shelves. Come and see."

It was easy to see what the big attraction was. Several large, bright illustrated adventures of Tintin were the nuclei of clusters of students; their bright eyes followed their fingers through the incredible exploits of the wimpy little hero. Those who were waiting for a turn at the coveted hard-backed cartoon stories had pulled other books off the shelves to while away the time—books that had been hitherto untouched. A young man sat on the floor, leaning back against the wall, his lips moving as he followed a description of the bone structure of the human body, and another was perusing a discussion of the Old Testament.

"Not being used to owning books, these children were in awe of them," Robby explained. "The Tintin books were a stroke of inspiration I had, and they've broken down the barrier of just feeling strange around books. The French language is not that well-known to these kids, anyway. They weren't able to make it into regular schools, like the Methodist Secondary School where your English classes are. Oh, hello, Morgan!"

Morgan Kenani, the teacher who had been one of the witnesses at our marriage and who now lived in the small house next to ours, came out of a nearby classroom. Being Zambian, or as he still insisted on calling himself, Northern Rhodesian, he spoke English. "Good morning, Robby!"

"It's afternoon now. Do you want a ride home with us? We're going home for lunch," Robby answered.

"Oh, no, I won't be eating lunch. My sister cooks for me, and we eat about five o'clock in the afternoon." Morgan's eyes looked tired and listless.

"Did you have breakfast?" Robby inquired.

"I had tea. But, really, the *ugali* fills me up at night. I'm really not hungry in the morning."

"Why don't you come on home and have a papaya or an avocado off our trees, Morgan? Some lemonade, or something? Something with vitamins in it."

"Oh, no, no. I don't eat fruit. I'm used to *ugali.*" Morgan made a self-deprecating gesture as if to ward off any more unwanted concern about himself.

"Do you know Baba Noah, the director at the Ruashi social center?" Robby asked at lunchtime.

I shook my head.

"He and I had a big problem to settle this morning. Or, I guess I should say it was he and his wife who had the big problem."

"If this story has to do with how big a problem wives are, I don't think I want to hear it," I cautioned him. "Not after all the trouble we went through to make sure you had a wife!"

He laughed. "No, the problem arose when the water was shut off to the Ruashi school. I was surprised because last week I had given Baba Noah seven zaires to go down and pay the bill. Seven zaires would be about fifteen dollars, or the equivalent of a month's salary of a teacher in the social center. Don't ask me how they survive on that, because I know a sack of corn flour for making *ugali* costs about seven zaires. But that's the going salary, and people seem glad enough to get it.

"Anyway, I called Baba Noah in and asked him about the seven zaires. It turns out that he had hidden the seven zaires away that night, awaiting the morning when the water company would be open. But the next day, when he went to get it, it was gone. Then his wife came in with a new piece of cloth, a new scarf, and new sandals. She told him that she needed those things, and that if he didn't let her keep them, she was going to pack up her pots and pans and go back to her father's house in the village."

We were quiet a few moments. I thought about the laundry bag of clothes stolen on our honeymoon and how little I was missing any of them.

"Robby . . ." I began.

"Yes," he answered.

"If I hadn't come out here, there's no way I would ever have understood what you see here. You once wrote and told me that a man's salary may be seven zaires a month—that one woman's outfit would require the whole seven—and that the sack of corn flour they need to eat is also seven zaires. My only conclusion was that you were exaggerating for effect, because it was impossible for a family to survive like that. Baba Noah's wife had to take matters into her own hands if she was to have clothes. I guess that explains the survival."

"Poor guy," said Robby. "That money has to be deducted from his salary for months to come and will make *those* months harder for them all."

We finished our meal in silence.

Weekends we looked forward to sleeping in as long as possible. For me, a morning person, that wasn't very long. I liked getting up to see the fresh carpet of violet-blue jacaranda blossoms drifted over the wide street like a magical highway. I liked to watch Friday bound along the hedge of bougainvillea like an antelope. I liked to cradle a cup of something hot in my two hands and make plans for the new day or remember the day before. But I soon discovered that slipping out of bed while Robby lay in profound slumber was a mistake of deadly proportions. I had assumed that if he was asleep, he wouldn't miss me. But the reproach in his face when he finally got up told me

164

that waking up to an empty pillow was not his idea of a happy marriage.

On this particular morning I lay poised in wakefulness. The fresh cool world was calling to me. But when I stirred, a heavy arm descended over me as if to say, "Don't even think of moving."

Suddenly there was a reverberating metallic sound. I slipped out from under the arm and into my robe. Again the noise sounded. I went out into the courtyard. Someone was banging on the big green metal door that opened into the back garden. That door had been opened only once or twice since we lived on Avenue Maniema, and I had no idea where the key might be.

"Who's there?" I called.

There was silence, and then a quieter knocking.

"Qui est là?" I tried in French.

There was another pause, and more knocking.

I went and stood in front of the tightly closed door. "Who is it, please?"

To my surprise, Morgan's polite voice replied, "It's Morgan. Please, I need to speak with Robby."

I explained that he was asleep. He apologized but said it was very important.

"Morgan, I can't find the key to this door and don't know how to open it. Could you come around to the front door, so we can talk without shouting?" I asked him.

"Oh, no!" he said quickly.

Mystified, I decided it was time to awaken Robby.

"Why does he insist on coming to the back door?" Robby grumbled. "That door is impossible to open." Taking the key, he went out into the courtyard. "Morgan, come around to the front door, please! I don't want to open this door."

165

"No, really, I couldn't do that," Morgan insisted, in an embarrassed tone.

Robby rolled his eyes and whispered to me, "He thinks only honored guests should come to the front door, and he simply won't do it."

"Morgan, will you please come around to the kitchen door, if you don't want to go to the front?"

There was a short silence from behind the door, and finally, ignoring the request, Morgan burst out, "Robby, it's very important. Excuse me, but thieves have broken into the storeroom at the social center."

Robby wrestled with the large key in the rusty metal lock. I couldn't help smiling in spite of the crisis at hand. Morgan had won. No, not Morgan. The winner was whoever had trained him to think that a white-skinned person was superior to him. I wondered how long it would take him to realize that we needed him as friend, neighbor, and colleague.

The thieves had apparently climbed a tree branch across to the roof, pulled up a section of tin, and dropped down into a classroom. Then, piling tables and chairs up high, they had crawled through the ceiling partition into the adjoining storeroom. There they took a typewriter and bolts of cloth destined for the use of the women's sewing classes and vanished.

Morgan, who carried the keys to the classrooms and storeroom and felt responsible, was really upset and insisted on bringing a friend to help him keep watch the coming night. He was sure the thieves would come back for more. Morgan's friend was a big brawny man armed with a mean-looking club, and, toward sunset, the two of them settled down on mats in the inner courtyard.

Around nine o'clock that night, Robby put aside the magazine he was reading and looked restless.

"Susan, do we have anything good to eat that I could take over to Morgan and his friend? I thought I'd drive over there and see how they're doing."

"I don't have any *ugali*, if that's what you mean," I answered. "Remember, Morgan said he doesn't eat fruits and things like that. But there is a big container of leftover spaghetti and meatballs that I could heat up. I just hope they like it."

I rode along the mile or so through the city night. The sweetish smell of burning charcoal mingled with the fragrance of flowers which were somehow blossoming before even the first rain of the season bathed their roots. The odors seemed no longer foreign, but familiar and good.

Robby got out of the car in front of the social center, whose entrance was lit by one dim yellow bulb. His soft desert boots made scarcely a sound on the cement as he turned the corner into the courtyard and neared the little shelter of cardboard and mats for the two guards during the chill of the night.

"AAAAAAAgh! Eh! Eh! Eh!" I heard the horrible shout in the darkness. *"Voleur! Mwizi!"* The French and Swahili words for thief rang through the night. I heard the crash of a club, and then silence.

By the time I reached the scene, it was over. There was the big brawny guard shaking his head and apologizing over and over to Robby. Morgan was wringing his hands in mortification that the guard, in the confusion of darkness, had mistaken Robby's quiet footsteps for the return of the thieves.

Robby's eyes were big. "Whew! I ducked just in time!" he said. "Suddenly this guy who seemed eight feet tall was towering over me with that club. I bet there's a crack in the cement where it landed."

He praised the embarrassed guard for being so

167

watchful and left the pot of meat and pasta. It may not have been the accustomed *ugali*, but when Morgan returned the pot in the morning—to the back garden door, of course—it was polished clean.

16
Shadows at Star Mine

I turned the faucet and glanced at the thicket of ferns and rock. A thin arc of water played up, tumbled onto the brown rocks, and bubbled over into the soil where the baby ferns were unfurling daily. Robby should be home from the office soon. I laid a plate of peanut butter cookies on the patio table. I had corrected all the ninth-graders' English exercises and felt ready for a break. Friday had her head resting on her forepaws in an alert position, ears cocked like a tiny jaunty hat. I looked at her fondly.

A Doberman Pinscher was the last dog in the world I could imagine myself owning, but this sleek little female, affectionate and bright, wasn't anything like the mean, lean dogs I had seen rattling their chains in someone else's yard. Part of it had to do with the way her ears had been cut; instead of streaking back in a flared, vicious line, somehow her ears stood up, with the ends flopping over comically. She worshiped the ground Robby walked on, and I could see that she was listening just as hard as I was for the sound of the motorcycle he used when someone else had the car.

There was a loud bark, and I saw Friday leaping at the door handle. Twisting her body and muzzle to bear down on the lever, she neatly opened the door into the kitchen and disappeared. Another thump, and I knew she had mastered the door out into the garage and was gone. Only then did I hear the faint purr of the distant motorcycle.

By the time I got outside, Friday was leaping all over Robby, who could barely support the motorcycle as he tried to close the gate. Morgan watched us from the steps of the small white house sheltered under tall pines. Trying to calm Friday down, we strolled around to greet Morgan.

"Good afternoon," he said. Beside him on the steps were a pair of shiny black shoes, toes pointed in the current European fashion.

"What's that you have there, Morgan, new shoes?" Robby teased. "I didn't know the social center paid *that* well!"

Morgan looked serious. "Buying them took my whole September's salary," he admitted.

"Well, how. . .? I mean, what. . .?" Robby stammered a bit.

Morgan seemed to understand. "I eat with my sister, you know, and I live here."

"Don't you sometimes buy meat or fish for your sister to cook, or bread, or. . . ." It was inconceivable that one would put everything into a pair of shoes that would soon crack and wear in the dust and concrete of this town.

"Next month I will," he said. "But *ugali* fills me up. I sleep well and wake up still satisfied."

"Morgan, you should have talked with me before you did this. I'm afraid you're not getting all the protein and vitamins you need, especially the days you look so tired at work. Why didn't you spend fifty makuta on a pair of plastic thongs, and use the rest for fish or vegetables or milk?"

170

Morgan slowly shook his head.

Robby went on eagerly. "Look at me. I'm the director, and yet I wear flipflops to the office when it's hot."

Morgan looked at Robby. "You can wear flipflops to the office because when people see your feet in thongs, they know that you have other shoes back home. But if they see me in thongs, they will know that it's the best I can do."

"Ah, I see," said Robby. "They are very nice shoes, Morgan."

Friday had disappeared, and we went calling around the house and then into the kitchen without hearing an answering bark.

"Where is that girl?" Robby wondered, and suddenly we heard the click of her toenails on the black tile floor. As she came through the kitchen from the courtyard, she deliberately looked to one side and avoided our eyes.

"She looks guilty!" I said.

We soon saw why. On the bricks of the patio lay the plate that had once held cookies. A few scattered crumbs explained the guilty look.

"I guess since she can open all the doors of the house, nothing is sacred," Robby said. "But isn't she clever—she knows when to push on a door and when to pull, depending on whether it opens in or out!"

I picked up the plate, thinking of how hard it was to find peanut butter in Lubumbashi. "As far as I'm concerned, the cookies were for us."

"We can do without a snack," Robby said. "It'll make us all the hungrier for our evening out."

Dave and Mary Jo Schmidt, a young couple in the Teachers Abroad Program at the secondary school at Mulungwishi, were coming to spend the weekend with us and take us out to eat that night.

"And tomorrow should be fun, too," I said slyly, with a glance at Robby to see how good he was at keeping secrets. The next day would be November second, my twenty-fourth birthday, and knowing Robby's ability to make special and surprising things happen, I couldn't wait to see what he had up his sleeve.

He was pretty cool. "Yes, I thought about taking a picnic lunch out to Star Mine and spending the day. I think I know where I could get some old inner tubes to take along."

"That does sound like fun," I agreed.

"What shall I wear?" I said later. I looked appraisingly at the pink linen dress with a boat neck and bell sleeves. I especially liked the little flowered lace trim on neck and sleeves.

"You want to borrow something of mine?" Robby asked, seriously.

"No! I don't want to borrow a khaki shirt, thank you," I answered. "Now if Sharon or Peggy were here, I might go through *their* closets. You know, the first time I ever went out with you, I was wearing a paisley skirt and jacket that belonged to Peggy. Do you remember that night—dinner at Chowning's Tavern in Colonial Williamsburg?"

"You mean the time my sister came home from school and told me that your sister said that you and I had a date? So I had to call you up and make a dinner date. I mean, if you thought it was a date. . . ."

"Why, Robby Ackerman, you asked me out yourself! You asked me if I wanted to go with you to a meeting of Inter-Varsity Christian Fellowship in Williamsburg, and I accepted. I call that a date!"

"I call it a ride," said Robby.

"So who said you had to take me out to a candlelit

172

dinner by the fireplace in an old Virginia tavern?" I said, indignantly. "From what your mother has told me, you wouldn't buy a girl a Coke if you didn't think it was worth your while. So don't tell me you didn't choose of your own free will to ask me out to dinner!"

He arched his eyebrows. "It was well worth my while, I'd say!"

"Oh, you're maddening!" I answered, but I couldn't help laughing. "We did have an awfully good time that night!"

It was past ten the next morning when I heard our guests stirring. I popped the coffee cake into the oven to warm up and poured the icy juice. I smiled to myself at Robby's poor little excuse thirty minutes before. He had mumbled something about looking for inner tubes down at the social center and that he would be right back.

I thought of the day I turned fifteen. I spent most of that day drenched in self-pity because no one had said happy birthday to me that morning. I myself had forgotten it in the rush of sleeping late and nearly missing the bus and only remembered it when I had to put the date on a paper in my first class. I was convinced that no one else in my whole family had remembered or would remember, and moped through the day. How dazzled I was at four o'clock in the afternoon, to come home to a houseful of friends, a cake, and a coveted new hi-fi record player with a Mozart and Beethoven record on it! They loved me after all.

As I poured the juice and plugged in the little electric tea kettle that had been a wedding gift, I felt a nostalgia for all my birthdays gone before and the family that had made me feel special. Now I had Robby.

The night before, we were sitting around a pot of sizzling oil on a white-draped table in the dim restaurant. Spearing bits of sirloin on our long fondue forks and cooking them one by one to perfection, Mary Jo, Dave, Robby, and I were enjoying the tasty sauces and relishes. Robby and Dave were talking about motorcycles. When I could get a word in edgewise, I decided to tell that little story about how I thought no one had remembered my birthday, laughing, of course, at the way I had really gotten into self-pity for a while. I thought our guests might be more comfortable seeing my surprise the next day if I had warned them that it would be my birthday.

"I'm glad we chose this weekend to visit you, then," said Mary Jo delightedly. "Birthdays are always fun!"

Robby's eyelids didn't even flicker as he turned back to Dave. "The B.S.A. motorcycles are British-made, of course, and the 175 cc bike I have is really all I need for going about town here. I've been looking for spare parts, but haven't had much luck."

I was impressed. How did he do that so smoothly? He actually looked as if he had never heard me say a word about my birthday, nor was it a subject that interested him.

I heard the motorcycle at the gate at the same time that Dave and Mary Jo came out onto the sunny patio. As Robby came in and said his good mornings to everyone, I discreetly looked down at the table I was arranging in case he had anything like flowers to surprise me with, but he unplugged the tea kettle. "This thing has been boiling for quite a while, it looks like," he said.

As I took the steaming kettle and began filling the brown teapot, suddenly Mary Jo started the birthday song. "Happy birthday to you. . . ."

Dave's deep voice joined in. ". . . Happy birthday to you!"

Mary Jo handed me a small package tied with a bow as they finished up gaily: "Happy birthday, dear Susan, happy birthday to you!"

I laughed happily. "Thank you! You two really caught me by surprise!" As I set down the kettle and began to untie the bow, I sneaked a quick look at Robby. He was standing silent and dumbfounded.

"Thank you, Mary Jo, Dave, for these beautiful hand-painted note cards," I said, and then I looked at Robby.

"Happy birthday, Susan," he said.

That was all? Happy birthday, Susan? I looked straight into his eyes. They looked back into mine with a mute apology. "I guess Dave and Mary Jo caught me by surprise, too. I'm sorry."

"That's okay, honey; going swimming at the mine pit will be a great way to celebrate!" I heard myself saying with a false bright smile. It may have been my twenty-fourth birthday, but inside I was a crushed and deflated fifteen once again.

An abandoned mine pit doesn't sound like the most beautiful place to swim and picnic, but this one certainly was. Mine de l'Etoile was a hole five hundred feet deep, where roaring front-end loaders and bulldozers used to bite the ore-rich rock out of the earth. This earth was so rich with copper and other minerals that even the slag heap by the refineries was said to contain four percent copper. Though most countries would consider that rich, the Congo could afford to let it stand while they scooped out the richer earth elsewhere.

Star Mine was no longer worked, and subsequent rainy seasons had filled the crater with sparkling blue water—a perfect resort lake, with not a single vacationer taking advantage of it except the four of us that Saturday afternoon. The heavy mineral content of the water kept algae from forming, and not a blade of grass or a bush grew in the tumbled rock and red soil that reached high above the water's edge.

Balancing the inner tubes and a picnic basket, we descended the side of the crater to find a picnic spot near the water. Little caves and mini-tunnels honeycombed the descent and beckoned us to explore. Here were the charred bones of a roast goat. In a cave were some crude iron tools. Robby explained that those who made malachite ash trays and eggs and jewelry came here to find chunks of the deep, green-black ornamental stone. When we were seated at last on a tiny peninsula jutting out into the cold blue water, dipping our feet before getting up the courage to dive into the frightening depths, Robby pointed to a cave opening far on the other side.

"Up there was where John and I discovered a cache of arms hidden away. It was near Christmas, soon after we had arrived here, and not long after the Katangese secession. National troops had been sent in to keep this province a part of the Congo whether they wanted to or not. But those very soldiers were the ones who were raiding the countryside for food and women and sometimes killing the inhabitants of whole villages. In Lubumbashi there were roadblocks everywhere, and we were stopped at every corner so that some soldier could satisfy himself that we weren't mercenaries hired by the rebels."

Robby stopped himself. "But I wrote you all about that in my letters, didn't I?"

"About the political situation, yes, but not about finding a cache of arms!" I said. "That sounds scary.

176

Were you able to get away from the cave without anyone seeing you near it?"

"Get away from the cave?" Robby laughed. "The hard part was carrying the four cases of hand grenades, bazooka rockets, artillery shells, and small arms ammunition out to the car."

I gasped. "You didn't take them with you!"

Robby shrugged. "We were good Boy Scouts. We knew it was the kind of thing you should turn in to the authorities."

Dave and Mary Jo groaned. "You know they could have shot you on sight!" said Dave.

"I know that now, but I was still pretty naive then," said Robby. "Somehow we got on into town without being stopped. We decided we'd have a little fun, so we parked the VW on the main street of town and carried a box of arms up the elevator to the apartment where Pat Rothrock and Mary Bozeman lived. 'Merry Christmas!' we said when they opened the door."

I winced at the macabre humor.

Robby laughed again. "They weren't any more amused than you are, Susan. In fact, the stuff frightened them to death. 'We're calling Ken Enright,' they said. 'He'll know what to do.'

"Ken was irritated with us for doing something so foolish, but he said to bring the stuff on over to his house and we could bury it in his backyard. Well, when we got over there with it—just a couple of blocks, you know—he took one look at the quantity of arms in the cases and shook his head. No way was he going to bury that much dangerous material in his backyard. Already there were people around who wanted his neck. That would be all they needed!"

"So you couldn't have approached a policeman or

soldier and asked them what to do?" I ventured. "Explained the situation?"

"And risk getting one that shoots first and asks questions later?" Robby shook his head. "Ken soon got that idea out of my head."

"So what did you end up doing with it?" Mary Jo wondered.

"We put the grenades and bazookas and ammunition into the trunk of Ken's car, and locked it. Then he gave me the key. He got into his car and drove out of town the other direction where there's a dam, a reservoir, and the power plant. I followed a bit later on my motorcycle.

"When the policemen stopped him at the edge of town, they weren't able to search the vehicle because Ken didn't have the key, and it didn't seem worth their bother to insist on his going home to get it. I followed his tracks to the far side of the lake—by this time it was dusk. We pushed the heavy cases out into the water. But heavy as they were, they still wouldn't sink. We tried to reach out and force them under, but they sailed away beyond our reach toward the dam."

"Don't tell me it blew up the dam!" I shuddered.

"I guess we would have found out if it did," Robby answered.

I turned to Mary Jo. "Now I know why he didn't tell me everything in letters."

The afternoon sun was warm, the sky blue, the crusty rolls and cheese were perfect. But when I swam, I stayed close to the edge of the crater. It wasn't just knowing how deep the mine was; it wasn't just the chill of the water; it was the shadow, too, of the risk and danger that life held. I breathed a prayer of thanksgiving that the naïveté of the two Paxmen hadn't been a fatal flaw.

178

That night Robby took me in his arms again to tell me happy birthday. "I'm sorry I forgot," he said. "You're the most special person in the world; I guess I'm so happy just being with you, that the calendar doesn't even seem relevant."

But I was past feeling like pouting. "I had just what I wanted—you. When I was remembering my fifteenth birthday, I had just gone back too many years. The birthday I'm remembering right now was November two years ago, when you had just arrived in Lubumbashi, around the same time as the story you told us out at the mines. I had been watching the mail for something special from you, but instead, there was nothing at all for weeks. It was a windy November second, cold and blustery, when I came home from class, half-hoping that some surprise would materialize, but willing to settle for a letter. Instead, Daddy handed me the front page of the Newport News *Times-Herald*: "Rebel Troops Marching on Lubumbashi; Americans Advised to Evacuate."

Robby laughed. "Yes, everyone fled to Zambia. Everyone except John and me. How could we afford to be evacuated on twenty-two dollars a month?"

"You're laughing," I said soberly. "But I was scared to death. I remember thinking how I didn't even want a birthday card, or a bouquet of flowers, or a new sweater, or anything but you. And you seemed so far away. I wondered if I'd ever see you again, if you'd survive getting sent to one of the world's hot spots."

"Ever think how brave you are to come and join me in that very spot?" Robby said gently.

I was quiet, surprised at the word *brave*. I thought again of Anne Lindbergh's words: After all, there he is and I've got to go. . . . *Brave* didn't have anything to do with it.

179

"Brave?" I teased. "Maybe crazy!"

"I'll tell you what was crazy," Robby said, snuggling closer. "It was crazy spending those two years apart. I can't imagine what we were thinking of."

17
The Dinner That Disappeared

I checked my recipe again: "Orange-Currant Sauce—For roast duck, lamb, ham, or chicken." The mixture of orange juice, cayenne pepper, and mustard dissolved in jelly looked just as nauseating as it sounded, but I thought Betty Crocker *knew!*

Well, there was the chicken, roasted to a golden brown. It looked all right, though that morning my desperate shriek had brought Robby running. Having chosen a nonliving, featherless hen from the French butcher shop in contrast to the flopping, cackling ones in the market, I wasn't prepared to flip the bird over to find her head, nicely plucked and white, staring reproachfully up at me from the end of the curved neck.

Yes, there was the chicken, now properly headless, thanks to Robby. And there were the homemade rolls, baked yesterday and warmed up in the oven with the chicken. But I had my doubts whether Bishop Shungu, our invited guest this Sunday evening, or the doctor and minister who had spent the weekend with us, were going to be excited about that Orange-Currant Sauce. I heard laughter coming from the living room, and I wondered what good story I had just missed. For the tales I was hearing around that dining table day after day I'd cook any amount of company meals, but couldn't they wait to share them until I got there? I wrinkled my nose at the bowl of reddish liquid. At least it would add color to the table.

"Hey, Susan, can I do anything to help?" Robby stuck his head around the corner of the butler's pantry that separated the dining room from the kitchen. "We'll have to leave in about thirty minutes to pick up the students."

On Sunday evenings we drove out to the university to pick up any English-speaking students who might wish to take part in our English church service.

"Sure, why don't you carve some meat off this chicken and carry it in? It'll save time at the table," I answered, going in with the basket of rolls and the bowl of runny currant jelly that reeked of mustard and pepper.

Chicken is an African delicacy, I thought with satisfaction, watching Bishop Shungu take second helpings, even if the red-currant sauce, ignored at one corner of the table, reflected Betty Crocker's Nordic bias. "Here, let me fill the platter again," I said, picking up the bare plate and the empty bread basket and heading for the kitchen, where the rest of the roast chicken lay on the counter.

Or in the oven? I searched the kitchen wildly. That chicken had to be somewhere! The counter was bare. The table was bare. Nothing but dirty pots and pans sat on the kitchen range. The oven was empty. Well, if there was no chicken, there should at least be bare bones. But not a bone was in sight. And the rest of the rolls? Where were they?

My eyes dropped to the floor. Still no chicken bones, but under the table was a suspicious-looking crumb of bread. And then I noticed the grease spots all over the black tile, some of them in a telltale doggy footprint shape. I whirled to see the back door slightly ajar. Friday had come and gone, leaving nothing behind her.

How do you go in to your guests and announce that the dog has just gobbled up their dinner? You don't, I decided. You take in the dessert and coffee and blame it on the need to hurry. Thank goodness Friday had yet to learn how to open the refrigerator, or even my mixed fruit bowl would have been in jeopardy.

After such an inauspicious introduction to pilot Harold Amstutz at our wedding, I was a bit uneasy to learn that we were to see him often in Lubumbashi. He and his red and white single-engine Cessna 206 were based up-country in Kapanga, but bringing people to and from Lubumbashi was part of his regular work. Often, before sunset, Robby would drive out to the airport and come back with Harold, whose aviation uniform was knee-length Bermuda shorts and a generous plaid sport shirt hanging far over his stomach. His jokes and stories were a lot more fun when it wasn't my wedding and honeymoon that were endangered. One of the big topics of conversation was his plan to fly from the U.S. across the Atlantic and down over half the continent of Africa with the new twin-engine Piper Aztec that Methodist churches back home were purchasing for his use in the flight ministry.

Before I knew it, I was looking forward to Harold's visits, and when his children passed through on their way to and from school holidays, it changed our empty dwelling into a home. Harold, Elsie, Debby, David, Scott, and Peggy arrived on the 20th of December, together with Elsie's mother from Virginia, and until

183

they flew on home to Kapanga on Christmas Eve, I had all the gaiety I needed.

Having a house full of children gave me the urge to make cutout sugar cookies in Christmas shapes. I thought I could find the cocoa to make fudge, too. And how about those yummy breakfast breads, all festive with nuts and cherries? Betty Crocker showed them in living color. As soon as school was over that Wednesday noon, with the holiday week to come, I mixed up the sweet-roll dough while Pascal cleaned up after the soup-and-sandwich lunch for the eight of us. But the sour smell of the yeast turned my stomach, and only the hope of some festive results kept me at the task until the lump of dough was oiled, turned, and tucked under its dish towel.

While it rose, perhaps I could lie down just for a bit. I was tired. I pulled my hand-stitched curtains across the windows and stretched out in the darkened bedroom. It was midsummer here below the equator, and though the rains had come to break the heat and bring cool nights, the afternoon sun lit up the garden like Virginia Beach in July. In such a climate, why even try to make things be like Christmas back home? Feeling hollow and depressed, I shivered and pulled the bedspread up over my back. A dark cloud seemed to envelop me and push me down, down, into a deep sleep.

"Susan, Susan, you've been asleep all afternoon."

I felt the edge of the bed tilt as Robby sat down beside me. When his hand touched my forehead, it felt cold and foreign. Perhaps, if I never moved again, or spoke, or opened my eyes, I could keep from knowing that I was sick.

"I don't want to disturb you," he said softly. "But Pascal's gone, and the kids look hungry, and there's something in a big bowl in the kitchen that has spilled over onto the counter. It's kind of runny and white and smells fermented."

My stomach lurched. Thinking of that over-risen dough removed all doubt. I was sick and knew it. The now-familiar weakness was invading my veins like the bubbling yeast spreading through and inflating the sweet-roll dough. I couldn't answer.

"Honey, you're awfully hot. Don't be sick again." Robby sat there in the dusk with me a few minutes, pulling the spread more smoothly over me, lifting the strands of hair that had stuck against my sweaty neck and stroking my two hands. The nerves in my finger tips hurt at his touch, but I didn't say so. I needed him there beside me. I felt tears pushing out the corners of my eyes and seeping silently into the pillow.

"Silent night, holy night, all is calm, All is bright. . . ."

From the evening star glowing above the courtyard, the clear notes seemed to fall. In my fevered state, I wasn't surprised, only deeply touched as the music pierced the haze of sickness and went straight to my heart. ". . .Sleep in heavenly peace. Sleep in heavenly peace."

"It's little Peggy Amstutz," Robby whispered. "Doesn't she sing like an angel?"

I don't know what the Amstutz family got to eat that night; I don't know what ever happened to that loathsome yeast dough; I don't know when it was that Dr. Karistianos bent over me with a hypodermic needle of healing quinine; I remember only that our little four-year-old guest went sweetly on with every Christmas carol she knew, singing to her dolls out in the courtyard, and I was comforted.

Christmas morning, I awoke to a silent house. My fever hadn't totally disappeared, but it left me well enough to think about what I was missing. I missed the sound of muffled footsteps, rustling paper, and low talking as Mother and Daddy put the final touches on the pile of gifts under the tree. They stuffed the last tangerines into the lumpy brown cotton stockings pinned to the back of the couch for want of a proper mantel piece. I missed the giggles and whispers of sisters gathered impatiently on one bed in the predawn darkness.

In a rational moment, Robby and I had decided that our Christmas present to each other would be to order the carving of an African "Last Supper" from the same artist that had decorated the church at Mulungwishi. But a Christmas morning without a single gift to open or to enjoy watching someone else open was so far from tradition that it was hard for me to recognize it as Christmas morning.

Suddenly I thought of something. Mustering the strength to slip out of bed and into my wax print caftan, I went into the study and pulled out the attaché case that had cost me so dearly at Patrick Henry Airport six months before. A full, spicy fragrance reminiscent of Williamsburg and colonial Christmases rewarded me as I opened it, rummaged through its contents, and found the slim brown box I was looking for. Bayberry candles!

I set the two tapers in holders by the fruit bowl in the dining room. The rich olive color of the candles added a depth to the golden flames. Besides the great gift to the world that the first Christmas brought, I had another gift I wasn't thinking of. I would go right in and wake him up, I thought, taking up one of the candles. Williamsburg bayberry would be the first Ackerman-Yoder holiday custom.

By noon, my fever had gathered force. But it was not going to keep me from sharing Christmas dinner with the other missionaries at Warren and Lois Jackson's house. I was too weak to change out of my African cloth robe into holiday finery, but Robby helped me into the car as I was. We drove through the sunlit streets.

Good smells and "Merry Christmas!" greeted us in the Jacksons' kitchen. There on the top of the stove lay pans of light white rolls ready to pop into the oven for browning. Lois Jackson, with her apron and her attractively graying hair, and the other women who brought dishes of savory foods, cakes, and pies seemed to take a heavy burden from my shoulders. I could curl up on the sofa, watch the children play with their Christmas surprises, enjoy the decorations, the manger scene, and the holiday atmosphere that I had yet to see that Christmas.

"See my pet roach, Uncle Rob? See him? I caught him myself!" Little Christine Jackson, who was four years old, proudly showed off her new pet. Confined to his jar on top of the refrigerator, the two-inch cockroach waved magnificent feelers above his head to show off. The creature was infinitely more interesting both to Christine and Robby than any Christmas gifts.

I was getting the attention and sympathy I needed, too.

"Susan, you've got to stop getting sick so often," said Lois. "You've been in the Congo six months now. You should be used to this climate. Makes me wonder if you're boiling your water long enough. You could be getting something from the water."

I sat there in guilty silence. It would be betraying Robby if I admitted that we drank our water straight from the tap. *He* maintained that the Belgians claimed it tested pure. The other Methodist missionaries took the position that one could never be sure from week to week that impurities were not getting into the water supply, and that to be safe, one must boil and filter all drinking water.

"The Congolese here are looking for an Ackerman baby before long," someone else remarked, saving me from any incriminating admission about boiling the water. "Why else would a new bride be feeling sick all the time?"

"A baby?" I asked in surprise. "They're going to be sadly disappointed."

"Well, you never know," they said, as we sat down to a lovely Christmas dinner for which I had no physical appetite at all but which would feed my aching soul.

18
Tea in the Garden

I was a teacher, and I knew it. My sisters had taught me my first word in a play school in Uncle Kenneth's molasses-fragrant feed room, using a brochure about calf feed in which they circled the word *it* for me to learn. I repeated a hundred breathless times, "I-T spells *it*, I-T spells *it*, I-T spells *it* . . ." and couldn't wait till the first day of real school so I could raise my hand and tell Mrs. Carper with pride, "I know how to spell *it*—I-T!" Perhaps it was her admiring response that sealed my fate and made school a favorite place to be.

I walked into the English classroom this Tuesday morning, struck by the chill, dusty smell of the bare room. As my class of fifty fourteen-year-olds rose to their feet, I was struck, too, by their politeness in chanting, "Good morning, Mrs.!"

"Mrs. Ackerman," I corrected. "In English you use the name with the title of respect. Repeat, please: Good morning, Mrs. Ackerman!"

They chorused, "Good morning, Mrs. Ackerman!"

"Good morning, class!" I replied and walked over to my desk. "You may be seated," I said as I made the appropriate gesture and got out my roll book. "Madimba, Bernadette. . . ."

I had nothing but admiration for the effort and attention of the students, who had English only two hours a week and who were learning it as perhaps their fourth language. There were not enough books for them all, and money for school supplies was scarce. But these were the lucky ones—these who had found a place in the secondary schools, certainly not a majority of the teenagers of Lubumbashi.

Still, I had been spoiled by what I knew of teaching school in Virginia—walking in to the smell of coffee in the mornings; a bouquet of flowers from somebody's garden sitting on my desk; reading "just one more chapter" of *The Secret Garden* after the long noon recess; parties with birthday candles that relit themselves. I felt a bit ashamed of myself. Maybe all I wanted to do was to keep on playing school all my life. This morning it was definitely work.

I tried to draw my mind back to the lesson of the day. I had already learned not to lightly assign an original composition. At the snap of the fingers, I would have two hundred grubby slips of paper with unreadable sentences upon which to pronounce individual judgment. No, today we would stick to the paragraph they had studied for dictation.

"Open your notebooks and get ready to write," I instructed. "Now, write this: 'The students . . . are studying . . . their English lesson.' "

Perhaps if I weren't sick half the time, I'd be able to think of something better than this. I inwardly thanked the students for not looking as bored as they surely must be. Where was I? " 'The chairs . . . are behind . . . the pupils' desks.' " I saw that I had skipped a sentence. It didn't matter. These dictations were long enough as it was.

I looked over the bent heads as the students spelled the words. They were strangers to me. We

190

hadn't yet played together, laughed together, created problems for each other. I didn't know what made them happy or what made them sad. Was this really teaching?

Late that night I sat at the desk in the study, working through the stack of thin, flat notebooks, counting the faults in the dictations. Robby was outside the door that opened into the cool courtyard, worrying with a broken bolt in his motorcycle. I knew that in about nine hours I'd be standing before my 7:30 class, and I wanted to have those dictations ready to go over. I was hurrying, but suddenly I stopped moving my red pen and frowned to myself.

"Robby?" I called. "Something's strange here."

There was no reply from the courtyard. Only Friday, who lay contentedly at my feet, lifted her head, raised her little brown eyebrows, and looked sympathetic.

I rose and poked my head around the corner. There sat Robby in despair, holding the butt of a bolt. "The bolt to the kick-start mechanism broke," he said tragically.

"Oh, honey, that's too bad. Can you find another one in town?" I sat down beside him with an English notebook on my knee.

"The bolt broke," he repeated, staring at the defective hardware.

"No replacement?" I asked.

"They aren't to be found in Lubumbashi," he admitted gloomily.

"And the bike won't run?" I asked, expecting the worst.

"Oh, it'll run," he said grimly, "if I get out into the street and run to push-start it, like half the other motorcycle owners do in town here."

I could tell that the method wasn't up to his standards.

191

"Oh, that's terrible," I sympathized. "This just isn't our night. Can I tell you what's happened to me? I'm not sure what to make of it."

He let the bolt fall to the brick pavement and, with an effort, turned to listen to me.

"You see this dictation? It's correct and very neatly done. But this third sentence: 'The teacher is standing in front of the blackboard.' I never dictated that sentence. My mind was wandering back to schoolteaching in Virginia, and somehow I missed it. And yet it shows up in eight of these notebooks. Do you think—you don't think they had copied it into the notebooks before I even gave the dictation, do you?"

"It's possible," Robby admitted. "Grades are really important here, and if they saw a way to be sure of a good grade, they may have copied."

I was indignant. Cheating! My well-behaved, eager-to-learn English students, cheating right under my very nose! Where was my French-English dictionary? What was the French word for "to cheat?" Lecturing them in English would be useless, and I would have to do some quick research to get my French lecture together.

Robby's laugh caught me in mid-flight. "Hey!" he laughed. "Don't take it personally. This happens in Virginia too, remember."

I stopped and gave him a sheepish look.

He went on. "Too bad you don't have a glass eye."

"A glass eye? Why?" I asked in astonishment.

"Some teacher coming through Lubumbashi told me what he did to keep students from cheating when he went out of the room during a test. He took out his glass eye and laid it on the desk, where it stared at them, never blinking. That's what you need!"

I laughed and decided not to take this all so seriously. I didn't need a glass eye. I needed some sleep.

Hours later, I dragged myself up out of an exhausted sleep, aware of something, but I wasn't sure what. Was it a kiss? I heard the click of doggy toenails, and felt the urgent wet lash of Friday's tongue across my face. Robby sat up, instantly alert. As soon as the silent watchdog had our attention, she slipped to the floor and out of the room. Robby followed through the dark house, and I too, at a skeptical distance. Friday would surely have barked at any intruder. I was too tired to follow a dog around the house in the middle of the night, just to play games.

In the darkness, my shoulder struck the edge of the dining room door. "Ow!" I complained.

"Sh!" was Robby's swift and unsympathetic response from the kitchen. "Come here, Susan, and look out the kitchen window. But be quiet!"

Friday's body fairly trembled at the door, but she still made no sound. Over Robby's shoulder, in the dim light from the bulb at the corner of the house, I could see two men in dark clothes, bending over the rear wheel of our car in the open garage. As we watched, there was the metallic ping of a hub cap falling to the ground.

Robby hesitated no longer. "Watch here," he told me, taking Friday with him into the courtyard and wrestling with the back door that, thanks to Morgan's dogged persistence, had become a little easier to unlock.

All the noise that Friday had been holding back burst forth now in a high, continuous yelping. She flew around the house after the thieves, a streak of deeper black in the black of night. Tools clattered to the ground; the men leaped up and made for the closed gate. How anyone could get up enough speed on that short driveway to clear the tall iron spikes on the top of the gate was a mystery to me, but the two thieves had no difficulty at all.

We opened the kitchen door to a grinning, panting Friday and covered her with hugs and caresses. "How did she know to be silent until we understood what was going on?" I marveled.

"She's a smart dog. And to think she's just eight months old!" Robby's voice was pleased and proud.

The next evening the familiar abdominal pain, fever, and weariness moved through my body once again—this time barely a week after recovering from the holiday episode of fever. After the broken sleep and excitement of the night before, the pressure of correcting all the dictations and deciding how to approach the cheating problem, the two days of teaching, it wasn't surprising that I was ill again, but neither was it welcome. Was this what the new year had in store for me?

Another shot of quinine. People came and went in my bedroom. Mary Ruth Reitz came with a cool slice of fresh pineapple. Robby and Ken Enright were talking seriously about stomach pain and the name of some unfamiliar town that started with *L*. I closed my eyes and half-dreamed of a bright green quart buttermilk carton. Hampton Heights Dairy. A cool, smooth sip of salty buttermilk was all I wanted. Maybe a couple of fresh saltines to go with it. I hadn't seen saltines in six months. Yes, a couple of saltines and a glass of buttermilk from a green carton. That was just what I wanted.

"Robby," I called. "Oh, never mind." I stopped myself just before asking him for the crackers and buttermilk. Of course, there were none to be had. We were here in Africa.

194

Robby was at my side. "Honey, tomorrow morning I'm going to drive you down to Zambia to find a doctor Ken knows—a really good doctor with lots of experience in the Congo. He's English. Try to get some rest now."

"Robby?"

"Yes, honey?"

"Maybe a hot dog. You know, Jess's Hot Dogs. A chili dog, with onions. I think I could eat one of those."

Robby stroked my hair. "You'll have to wait a while for a hot dog from Harrisonburg's town square. So why don't you go off to sleep, and tomorrow Dr. Mason will have a look at you."

The next afternoon Robby drove back a hedge-lined lane in the attractive Zambian Copper-Belt town of Luanshya. As he pulled the car to a halt, I had an impression of lush green and fantastic rainbow colors. Where was I? Hollyhocks stood quaintly on guard, and roses graced symmetrical plots. On the close-cropped green turf before me was the very picture of an English tea garden. A chaise lounge, a few sun chairs grouped around a lace-draped table, and a tea tray complete down to the knitted cozy cuddling the teapot and a heap of fruit buns in a napkin-lined basket.

Though I was still too sick to appreciate what was happening, I was to learn later that precisely at half past three each day, Dr. Mason came home for tea from his work at the hospital that served the local copper mines. Neither Dr. Mason nor his wife, though their distinguished gray hair placed them close to retirement age, had slowed their pace in the slightest. Having worked as medical missionaries with the Plymouth Brethren for years, they now added a ministry of their own to his hospital work and her regular teaching. This ministry was to take in and lovingly bring back to health any stray person that was referred to them.

That afternoon, however, there was no tea for me in the garden. Before I knew it, I was lying between crisp cool sheets in a delicately floral bedroom. Ruffled bedspreads and piles of fluffy pillows made the twin beds look as if intended for a couple of princesses to while away a restful afternoon. There were soft throw rugs and sheer curtains fluttering gently over the long windows opening out over a second garden.

The fever already seemed to be losing its grip. I sat propped up on pillows and balanced a light tray on my knees, taking the first food I had had for days. I forgot all about chili dogs and buttermilk as I picked at bits of delicate white roast chicken from a bone china plate. Dr. Mason sat in an easy chair beside me, asking questions and putting together a picture of this baffling illness.

"We'll do tests at the hospital tomorrow," he said. "For now, why don't both of you get some rest? If you feel like it, at ten o'clock we have hot drinks in the living room. Breakfast is at seven."

Robby didn't move. Though not a princess, he had stretched out on the other twin bed and was fast asleep. I hadn't realized how hard this recurring illness must have been on that new husband of mine. It was well into the third day of our stay at Dr. Mason's before Robby left his bed for any other reason than to enjoy Mrs. Mason's exquisite meals.

"Well," Dr. Mason said several days later. "I can think of nothing else to test. You seem perfectly healthy. Even the fever has gone down to almost nothing."

My heart sank as I sat there on the examining table. Was he going to send me back to Lubumbashi with no help at all? Back to another week of teaching, back to the next episode of fever?

"When I tested your blood," he said, "it was healthy in every way. And though your Lubumbashi doctor said you had typhoid fever, it isn't possible. There's a certain characteristic clumping of cells in the blood after typhoid fever, and I don't find it here."

"Well, what about malaria?" I asked.

"Once the high fever has passed, it's impossible to detect malaria in the blood," he answered. "However, my opinion is that you are very susceptible to malaria, and that's what's giving you trouble. The abdominal pain is not unknown with malaria, though not really common, either. You must watch, young lady, not to let yourself get too tired and run down. And don't forget to take your weekly prophylactic."

"Oh, I never forget that," I assured him. "I take Daraprim regularly." Though what good it did me, I couldn't say.

They insisted we stay and recuperate a few more days. I drank in the spiritual beauty of the gracious couple as well as the loveliness of home and garden. The house ran like a beautiful piece of machinery. Crusty toast standing up in little English racks greeted us on the dot of seven in the morning, to be enjoyed with coffee and homemade marmalade—"The secret is in the bitter Seville oranges," said Mrs. Mason as she shared the recipe with me.

The house rang with her lilting call, "Oh, Special!" when she wasn't away teaching nutrition and health. What did she mean by "special"? I wondered that first day from back in the guest bedroom. But the second morning, when a handsome young man in a

197

white jacket brought me a tray with a drink and cookies precisely at eleven o'clock, it dawned on me that *he* was Special. With Special's help in the shining kitchen, it seemed that we were always eating. A lovely omelet and potatoes at 1:00, served in that haphazard dishing-out the English use instead of passing the food around the table in an orderly way; tea in the garden precisely at half-past three; meat and vegetables and dessert at seven; and then the 10:00 p.m. ritual of tea, coffee, or Milo—a malt-like drink with the texture of creamy hot chocolate.

It felt so good to be children in a nurturing household, but we were twenty-four years old, and we had work to do back in Lubumbashi. The Masons would take nothing for all their care and expense. On top of that, Mrs. Mason bundled up for us five jars of her homemade marmalade, three bottles of tomato chutney, and a round brown smoked ham, the likes of which were unknown in Lubumbashi.

There are people who give because they are made to give, like a tree in blossom that touches each passerby with its refreshing fragrance. Is it a gift from God, or is it a cultivated discipline of the spirit? I wondered. As we drove out of Luanshya and north to the Kasumbalesa border, Robby and I agreed about one thing.

"When we're in our sixties," I said, "I hope we'll be just like the Masons."

"I'm not sure you'll find me showing up on the dot for teatime," laughed Robby, "but I dream of having a home and family that other people will enjoy, too."

My mind went ahead to our home on Avenue Maniema. Maybe there with the black floors, bare turquoise walls, and scratched white Melmac plates, we were undergoing training for just such a future. We had been well-furnished with role models this week, I thought.

19
Shattered!

"Robby, I don't want to go!" My nose stung and my throat ached with the effort not to cry. My favorite red-and-gold dress, nicely folded, was suspended over the open suitcase, but I couldn't drop it in. Here was my second chance to enjoy Victoria Falls, and all I wanted to do was get back in bed and pull the covers over my head.

"Why don't you want to go?" Robby stopped folding shirts in surprise.

"My students are never going to learn English!" I wailed.

"You didn't say that earlier today when you asked the director for time off to go on a business trip with your husband," Robby reminded me.

"But I felt fine then!" I stopped suddenly, guiltily. I wasn't supposed to be sick any more, after all the attention I'd had, but this afternoon I felt weak and hot again. It was as if a virulent dye were spreading through my veins, blackening my emotions as well as making my body wilt like a hibiscus flower torn from the branch.

"Why don't you lie down and let me finish the packing? Maybe you'll feel fine in the morning." Robby looked as though he didn't quite believe in his own optimism. "But you have to go with me. I've got

200

to drive Bill and Doris Davis down to Lusaka where they'll catch a flight to Botswana for a conference and then I have to wait there for them till they come back at the end of the week. Since hotels are so expensive in Lusaka, we'll drive on down to Livingstone. You and I can stay so cheaply in one of those thatched-roof houses that it would be worth the drive. You have to come, Susan. I won't be able to enjoy those Falls without you, and I can't leave you here to be sick alone."

Slowly I dropped the dress into the suitcase.

The next morning, as we drove toward the Kasumbalesa border, it helped to have Bill and Doris Davis along. Bill was full of stories from his years as an African bush pilot, and Doris, a dainty little woman who taught women's cooking and sewing classes, had a lively sense of humor, too. Laughing with them kept my mind off the fever, which had not abated in the least after a restless night.

The Congolese customs agent appeared unusually glad to see us drive up.

"I've been wanting to see you," he said close to Robby's ear.

"You have?" Robby asked politely. "You mean ever since I gave you a ride a month or two ago?"

"Yes," he went on. "It's about, you know, what you had in the car with you."

"School supplies?" Robby guessed, innocently.

The man looked from side to side and threw a glance over his shoulder before leaning closer. "The human skeleton. I found out later that I made a mistake. I needed the name of the dead person, the date he died, and what nationality he was."

Robby's eyes widened, but he said nothing.

"Most important, I needed to know what . . . he . . .

died . . . of!" This last was whispered in a tone heavy with significance.

I'm not sure how the customs agent interpreted Robby's continued speechlessness. But he went on with an air of conspiracy. "No one else knows, so I decided that if you keep quiet about it, I'll let it go this time. But, remember, the next time you try to cross this border with a human skeleton, you *must* have a certificate of death and identity papers."

Robby solemnly promised to be legal and above board with all human skeleton traffic in the future, and we were on our way.

"At least it gives us something to laugh about," I said, and we all agreed. It was not a laughing matter, however, that this border with Zambia was the route by which much of the mission's school and medical supplies entered the country. Recognizing the value of these institutions, the central Congolese government had granted the Methodist Church exemption from import taxes.

But even with the proper papers, try explaining that to the one or two lone officials in this isolated outpost surrounded by African bush. They had been trained to tax imports from Zambia, and tax imports they would. Missionaries devised ingenious ways to disguise their purchases, not in the interest of deceiving the government, but simply to claim their right to tax-exempt status.

"One missiouary brought a sixteen-foot boat in on top of his car one day," Robby told us as we drove along.

"How in the world could he disguise something that big?" I wondered.

"When the agent asked him what he had bought in Zambia, he waved his hand and said, 'It's all up there in my luggage carrier.' The customs agent climbed up and peeked into the bottom of the boat, where there were two boxes of groceries. He asked for the value of the groceries, charged taxes on that, and let him go on."

A few miles further on, Robby laughed again. "Another time I drove up to the border with sixteen beautifully lit-up taillights across the back of my car. The agent admired the display, inspected the empty trunk, and waved me on through with the fourteen spare taillights and the extra muffler I was bringing in from Zambia for mission vehicles."

I could appreciate the ingenuity it took to survive in such circumstances, but it was a game for which I had had little practice. I would leave it to those who could padlock honeymooners into their cottage, plant alarm clocks in nuptial ferns, or plot a secret aerial getaway from the scene of a wedding. I would leave it to the only person I knew who could have convinced me to come to this continent.

I smiled at Robby's profile; he must have been amused by his own thoughts. He didn't see my smile as he drove on through the green-gold grasses of late summer in Africa. But I felt it linger on my flushed face. If I had to be sick, this was as beautiful a place to be as any, I thought. We overtook a team of long-horned cattle pulling a cart piled high with sacks of charcoal. The sacks were so full of the charcoal that dried grass stalks had been woven in a lacy mesh to the sack opening to hold in its generous, rounded heaping. Three little boys in earth-colored shorts leaped out of the grass brandishing homemade bows and arrows at us, laughing themselves silly as they pounded a victory dance into the dust of our fleeing vehicle.

The next afternoon we left our passengers at the Lusaka International Airport with promises to pick them up there on their return from Botswana. Then Robby and I headed out of town toward Livingstone. It would be a long six hours, I knew, on that dreaded gravel road where meeting a car required a mutual giving up of half a lane—two tires on dirt and two tires on gravel. At the speeds people traveled here—as we well remembered from our honeymoon—driving was risky and required intense concentration. With Robby's driving tension and my fever of 102 degrees, I wasn't expecting much in the way of jolly conversations in the front seat of the Peugeot station wagon.

I slumped in the seat with my back to Robby, looking out the window. Mazabuka was the first real town. In Mazabuka, Asian shops marked General Traders sported turquoise, orange, red, and yellow columns on their front porches, brightening up the dustiness of the landscape. Leaving the small town, we passed a roadside stand of melons and fruits. Farther on, a spreading tree bore a sign that said "Butchery." A cowhide was tacked up to dry, and hunks of meat hung from the tree branches. I didn't see many clients, but then it was siesta time. Maybe I could sleep a while myself.

I closed my eyes, feeling the left side of the car leave the gravel strip to make way for an approaching car. Suddenly there was a loud "Thunk!" on the windshield. My eyes flew open to see the road before us vanish in a veil of gray lace. With a soft exclamation, Robby blindly guided the car to a stop on the shoulder. I whirled in my seat to look behind us; the car whose swift tires had flung the stone at our windshield was disappearing nonchalantly around a far bend in the road.

"He didn't even see what he did!" I wailed. Robby gave me a humorless smile and got out to inspect the damage. The flying missile had shattered the safety glass into a million snowy jigsaw puzzle pieces, all still attached to each other and their inner plastic lining.

"Well, I certainly can't drive with this in the way," Robby said. He pushed against the ruined windshield, and the glass crumbled harmlessly down across the dash, onto the floor and over the front seat.

"You can't drive without it, either, can you?" I asked. My voice trembled, and the sides of my cheeks ached with the effort of keeping my face from crumbling into tears.

Robby's voice was very businesslike, almost pleased. How did horrible things like this always leave him cool as a chameleon, while worrying about what *might* happen made him nervous as a jackal? "We'll *have* to drive without it. It's two o'clock on a Sunday afternoon. Even if Mazabuka, or Choma, or Pemba had a garage with a windshield that fit, it wouldn't be open on Sunday afternoon. Lusaka wouldn't have anything open, either. We might just as well ride on to Livingstone this afternoon. Then we can be where we want to be while they fix the car."

Ride two hundred miles without a windshield and with a fever of 102? He must be out of his mind! I would have collapsed against the khaki front of his shirt in tears, except that he had turned away. Instead, I sank down in the grass beside the road and buried my head in my knees for a few silent sobs, while Robby rummaged in the trunk for his whisk broom and started tidying things up.

He whistled a dry, tuneless snatch of music as he whisked the last bits of glass from the edges of the empty hole. "It'll be just like riding in a convertible," he said. "I've always wanted my own convertible."

I sniffed a little and then laughed in spite of myself. "A convertible is just the opposite of this," I protested. "It has a windshield and no top. We have the top and no windshield. That's not quite the same thing."

"Well, then, it's like a big motorcycle we can both ride on the front of!" he suggested. "But we'd better be prepared. We're bound to have some thunderstorms this afternoon. And there'll be bugs." With great relish, he put on his wine-colored wind-breaker, tying the hood so that only his eyes, nose, and mouth were visible. Then he handed me an extra long-sleeved shirt. "Put it on backwards," he said, "and you've got a scarf, haven't you?"

Thus protected, Robby started off gingerly at first, as the fresh warm wind strengthened against our faces, then gradually picked up speed. I felt so vulnerable, but at the same time exhilarated by the wind and the vulnerability. How near the landscape was! I was part of it! When I turned to look at Robby, whose sunglasses covered up most of the space left by the tightly pulled hood, I couldn't hold back a laugh. "You look hilarious!" I shouted against the noise of the rushing air.

"So do you!" he shouted back. I had forgotten how good it felt to laugh together.

Ahead of us a tall boy came walking down the middle of the road, strumming a guitar made from a milk can and strips of leather. As he moved to the edge of the road, he tucked the guitar under one arm and waved to us, opening and closing his fingers to signal that we had our lights on. Leaning forward and thrusting my hand through the nonexistent windshield, I playfully returned his signal. He let his arm drop and jumped back into the grass with a startled laugh. The missing windshield would be good for a lot more laughs as we drove on south that afternoon.

"I see now why this *isn't* just like riding a big motorcycle," Robby said a little later, as he slowed down and pulled off the road again. "A motorcycle lets the bugs go on by. We're just scooping them up. I've got to get rid of the ones that are crawling up my pants leg."

Apparently the bugs were being whisked into the car by the wind. The ones that missed bombarding our faces smacked against the back windshield, fell to the floor, and then came crawling forward to investigate the two human beings in the front seat. Every thirty minutes or so, Robby found it necessary to stop the car, get out, and shake the most curious ones out of his pants legs.

It was no use to hope for a dry afternoon in the middle of the rainy season. We hadn't gone far before the clouds began to play games with us. Great heavy-bottomed bullies and wispy, fluffy-headed waifs put their noses together and then scattered and regrouped across the sky like schoolchildren on the playground at recess time, plotting mischief. A fat cold raindrop whacked against my cheek, and another, and then a barrage of them, adding their own natural velocity to the speed of the vehicle.

There was nowhere to hide. The full force of a tropical rain slammed into the moving vehicle, into the gaping hole left by the crumbled windshield.

Robby slackened his speed. "Should I turn on the windshield wipers?" he joked against the sound of the torrent.

"Maybe on your sunglasses!" I shouted back. Rain

splashed off our faces, ran down our arms, soaked our jackets; beetles, grasshoppers, crickets, and tiny bees began to slosh around our feet in a steadily rising flood. At first, the shock of the icy water against my feverish skin had me gasping and fighting the onslaught; but before long all I felt was a warm glow under the refreshing shower, as the shock of diving into a cold pool dissipates with the warming energy of a brisk swim.

And then it stopped. Suddenly the afternoon sun was burning in our faces once again. A fresh, warm breeze, fragrant with the smell of washed grasses and some flowery perfume, whipped and teased our soaked jackets dry in a matter of minutes.

We drove through six of those showers before reaching Livingstone. What was left of the tired, gray clouds was sinking like a heavy iron lid on the swirled orange and rose of the sunset as we drove into the town. Robby pulled the wounded vehicle to a stop in front of a shop marked "Chemist." It was so quiet when he turned off the engine. No bugs, no wind, no rain; just the pounding of my heart and the prickling of my still-fevered skin. I peeled back my scarf; my hair was plastered and dried against my head.

"How do you feel?" Robby asked, turning to look at me.

"Well, I made it!" I tried to be nonchalant. "But I'm quite sure that six rainstorms and four hours of wind in the face aren't the cure for malaria!" This fever was like a new member of the family that I had finally accepted. We would spend our lives together.

Robby looked at me for a long time. "Wait here," he said in a determined voice, and disappeared into the pharmacy.

When he came out again, he tossed a packet of cellophane-wrapped pills to me. "Susan, we just can't have you spending your whole year in Africa with a constant fever. We've taken all the doctors' advice, and you're no better. I feel like you need to take something other than Daraprim once a week to prevent these malaria attacks, so I got these 100-milligram tablets of Nivaquine. Take one of them every single day, starting right now." He fished a water bottle out from under the seat, wiped off the bugs, and handed it to me. "Now."

It was a historic moment. With that first little pill, the disease was on the retreat. It may sound incredible, but as we settled into our thatched-roof rondavel by Victoria Falls that night, I felt wellness spreading through my body. It was as if the Nivaquine were neutralizing that powerful dye that had colored my existence, and I could feel its healing path in my veins. Thanks to Dr. Robby, I had seen my last malarial fever of the year.

For the next few days, while the car was being made as good as new, so was I.

The world held a sparkle I hadn't seen for months. Early in the morning, the two of us explored the paths at the edge of the great Zambezi and circled around the rim of the falls themselves, never tiring of the rush and boom of the water. As the lacy spray spread and plummeted through the air, it seemed paradoxically to stay where it was—the form and spirit of the falls were one, though each individual drop of water plunged on to its fate and was replaced by the next free-falling drop. And watching, I sensed the greatness of the form and spirit of which I, like the drop of water, had a part. Happy I was that my free fall from birth to death allowed me a glimpse of this great act of nature, a sacrament of love and beauty to carry with me down into the chasm of life.

One morning we got a ride into town to pick up the car with its brand-new windshield. I felt brand-new myself, and had a sudden inspiration.

"Robby!" I said. "Let's find that souvenir shop again and see if they have any more of the elephants to replace our stolen one."

They did. There was even one with a broken fighting tusk and a blackened digging tusk. There was the same dusty, tired look about this second elephant, as if the weight of seasons of dust baths lent a patina that a shiny waxed figure could never have.

Out on the street again, I couldn't resist peeling back the paper wrapping on the carving and taking just one more quick look at my symbol of Africa. It seemed to hold a promise, but I wasn't sure what it was. I only knew that it made me happy inside.

"Oh, look, a bakery!" I cried. "Let's get some things and have a picnic." With the flight of those malarial parasites, my appetite had come rushing back. I chose some pale biscuitlike buns, a few slices of cooked meat, a tiny tube of mayonnaise, and, farther down the street, a couple of ripe tomatoes and a Granny Smith apple for each of us.

"And now let's drive down along the Zambezi, upriver from the falls, you know, around where we took our honeymoon launch to see the sunset," I urged.

Robby's lack of enthusiasm puzzled me. Silently, he drove into the vine-draped woods, past the warning signs with the elephant and hippo pictures, for all the world like directions to the Africa section of the Washington zoo. Installed under a spreading baobab tree, I eagerly set out the lunch. I would fix Robby's

210

sandwich first. After all the trouble it was to get here, I hoped from the bottom of my heart his problem was hunger, not boredom. I lathered a split biscuit with the mayonnaise, laid on a slice of meat and one of tomato, and handed it to Robby before I made the same for myself.

I had never tasted anything so good, I thought, munching away, with my eye on that rare green apple. How wonderful it was to enjoy food again! A slight motion caught my eye. I turned to watch Robby laying down his sandwich with only one bite gone.

"I can't eat this," he said faintly.

"What's wrong with it?" I asked in surprise.

"I just can't eat it," he repeated. "Something about the mayonnaise and that bread."

The bread was new, and the mayonnaise tart and fresh. You could eat it if you weren't so picky, I thought, offended. What did he expect on a camping trip? Filet mignon? Could this be the same person who had chowed down all that dusty dry wedding cake? Digested those horrid, heavy "hamburgers" from the drive-in in Kitwe for breakfast? I gave up.

"You should have chosen the picnic items, I guess," I answered with an edge to my voice.

He gave me a helpless, pleading look. How could a helpless, pleading look be simultaneously so stubborn and obstinate?

"I'd like to go back to camp," I said. That wasn't exactly true. I didn't feel like being at the camp, or anywhere else in Africa with Robby, but least of all here at the site of the ruined picnic. The morning's sparkle had left the landscape, and all around us heat waves rose up from the steaming vegetation to agitate the clouds gathering for the afternoon shower.

"Don't be angry with me, Susan," Robby said. He

211

put his arms around me. His cheek against mine was fiery hot. Quickly I felt his face, his hands.

"Robby, are you sick? You're burning up!"

For the three remaining days of our stay in Livingstone, it was Robby's turn to have fever and nausea. Repentantly, I threw out the picnic lunch and rummaged for thermometer, aspirin, and alcohol. Being nurse instead of patient had its advantages. One evening I walked alone to the splendid hotel, the Mosiatunya, to dine on crisp salad and broiled fish. On the last afternoon, while Robby slept in the shuttered rondavel, I sat on a rock with a view of the Zambezi and wrote letters. Hopefully watching for the leathery back of a crocodile, or the tiny teddy-bear ears of a submerged hippo to add some drama to my correspondence, I saw only a yellow lizard soaking up the sun and a dirt-colored toad squatting at the edge of the path. Not even the baboons thought me worth menacing as they fed in the distant shrubbery and hurled insults at each other and their offspring.

Putting aside my stationery as the light suddenly weakened, I sat there through the pink-and-blue sunset, watching the mild-mannered palm trees and baobabs put on their dark evening cloaks and shrug their suddenly sinister shoulders. Strange new winds rose to whisper and bend the trees. Was I only imagining this, or did the roar of the falls grow louder and more thunderous with the sudden fall of night? I felt my eyes strain and widen to catch a cheery light somewhere, but there was none across the dark river, none behind me in the rondavel.

Suddenly I blinked and looked again to the east, past the thunder of the chasm. A scrap of polished copper flashed at me, like the warm glow of sun on the Vanhee's copper plates in the Lubumbashi afternoons. From between the far trees, the burnished moon rose steadily, winking through the branches until it cleared the earth and burned alone, round and molten from the refinery of the heavens. I snatched up my letters and stumbled over the uneven ground to the room where Robby lay. It was a moon to be shared.

Two days later found us once again on the road north from Lusaka with Bill and Doris Davis in the backseat of the car. Robby was a bit shaky, but the fever was gone, and he had kept his breakfast down. It was a relief to see the nicely paved two-lane road stretching ahead of us back to Lubumbashi. The windshield incident had confirmed my distrust of those "shared-lane" gravel types.

With the British-influenced traffic system, Robby had to master the art of driving down the left side of the road with the steering wheel at the left instead of on the right as they were in the Zambian vehicles. This kept him constantly alert, and I, sitting on the right where most Zambian drivers were, attracted some strange looks if I shut my eyes and laid my head back for a rest. I preferred to help Robby watch traffic anyway.

We were back in termite-hill country. The rocklike protuberances came right up to the road in places. I half expected around some bend to find that one of the red-orange mountains had reared its head right through the tar and gravel of the paved road. Cornfields, sorghum fields, and patches of young sunflowers crowded the shoulder in places; here and there I was happy to see stands of young pine trees, obviously part of a reforestation project. On the corner of one such stand of trees, the bottom branches and trunks were burned black, mute witness to a runaway grass fire. Such grass fires might be the only way to manage clearing and cultivation of African savanna land, I thought, but they were death to pine tree farms.

Chugging up the road toward us on our right came a black, lumbering truck piled to its limit with passengers, goats, and farm goods. Thick diesel smoke boiled out of its exhaust, nearly hiding the crowded taxi that was right behind, chafing at the slow speed of the big vehicle.

We all noticed that taxi. "He doesn't look like he wants to wait till we get by," I said, feeling somehow anxious at seeing the white nose of the taxi edge around the truck, then draw back, edge around again, then draw back.

"This is why I drive with the lights on," Robby said soothingly. "He can't help but see us." We hurtled on down the left-hand side of the road at sixty miles per hour, as the truck approached.

Suddenly my heart lurched in fear. Deliberately, determinedly, the taxi swung out into the lane before us and headed around that truck, rushing straight toward the front of our car. There wasn't time to think, only to react. While Doris screamed in terror behind me, Robby whipped the steering wheel to the left. For an instant, we were three abreast—the huge truck in the far lane, the taxi in our lane, and where were we? On a shoulder blessedly free of termite mounds, pine trees, and grain-fields, we skirted the certain rendezvous with death, and in an instant were driving once more on the straight paved road stretching empty before us. Doris's horrible scream echoed in the car. We were almost too shaken to go on.

Robby's eyes were wide. "I can't believe I actually whipped this wheel to the left. My years of right-hand driving should have made me want to avoid traffic by going right."

Bill Davis added, "And to have a clear shoulder, when all along there's been woods and scrub—thank God for that!"

We were still sober when we stopped behind a lone vehicle in front of the last barrier before Lubum-bashi—Congolese immigration at Kasumbalesa. Sundown was at hand, and we were anxious to be home. A show of passports and we should be a mere three hours from home.

But there was no one at the post, not even a woman with a cooking pot or a small boy with his "remote-control" vehicle. Languidly, a man opened the door of the vehicle in front of us.

"I've been here an hour," he said, "and there's been nobody here."

"Well, this is impossible," said Bill Davis. "We can't wait here until somebody decides to come to work. We've got to get through."

The other man, a Zambian, shrugged. "It's the time of day when a man needs a drink. I believe the officer is having his beer up the road at the building there on the left."

Bill almost spluttered. "He's left his post to go have a beer? He can't do that! Robby, let's go after him."

My heart sank at the very idea, but Robby needed no second invitation. While Bill raised the red-and-white-striped barrier, Robby drove through. It was only two hundred yards or so to the small building marked across with the dripping blue letters for Bar. Loud music in unfamiliar rhythms tumbled out the door as the two men opened it and disappeared inside. I wanted to hide.

In a few minutes, Bill and Robby came calmly out,

215

got back in the car, drove back to the barrier. Bill lifted it with the ease of an expert; Robby drove around the Zambian's car, turned, backed into his original place, and then sat docilely in line with a casual air.

"What happened?" I couldn't help asking.

"He was in there drinking with his superior from Kinshasa—but he'll be here in a minute," Bill said, his eyes twinkling. "His boss raked him over the coals for leaving the gate unlocked."

Here came the officer, fuming and sputtering, his shoulders hunched and his fists clenched. The Zambian gathered courage and presented his papers. I cringed as the agent slammed the papers to the floor and began to harangue the man in some local African language. Another car drove up behind us. Oh, let them go next, I prayed silently. Maybe his temper will sweeten by the time he gets around to us. But as soon as the Zambian had picked up his papers, saluted respectfully, and miraculously went on his way, Bill and Robby eagerly took his place.

The French flew faster than I could catch it: the words for barrier, bar, and law-breaking were obvious. Robby apologized but explained that they were not trying to escape the formalities, but rather trying to go through with them. Bill went farther than that. Raising his voice to match the voice of the agent, he began to draw dramatic comparisons between "before independence" and "after independence." Was that hitting below the belt? I wondered. Independence was only ten years old, still in its raw youth.

The agent knew how to stop the flow of words. Pointing to Robby's slim briefcase, he interrupted Bill abruptly. "Open this bag!" he ordered.

"But I've just been through customs," Robby protested. "This is immigration!"

The man insisted. "You must open that briefcase for inspection."

"But, sir. . . ."

I wondered why Robby protested so. To my knowledge, there was nothing in the briefcase but our travel papers.

"I have the right to inspect whatever you have," the agent said with relish. "You can't go unless you open it."

Slowly, Robby swung the case up onto the counter and snapped open the lock. Crumpled in the bottom of the empty case was his last clean pair of underwear and a tube of toothpaste. There was a silence, and then the agent slowly stamped our papers and handed them back.

When we were on our way again, I asked Robby, "Now why the big fuss about opening up the briefcase?"

"It gave him a bigger battle to win," he answered. "Did you see how friendly we all were in the end, all the handshakes, and see you next time, and bon voyage? We have our ongoing relationship to think of!"

"Well, we're all legal and aboveboard," I said. "The only thing we bought was the precious old elephant. . . ." My voice trailed off. "Robby, where is that elephant? I don't remember seeing it since our picnic by the Zambezi the day you got sick."

"Well, it must be in the car somewhere," Robby insisted.

But it wasn't. It wasn't in the suitcase; it wasn't in the trunk; it wasn't under the seat. The mysterious old elephant was gone without a trace. For the second time, the symbol of Africa had eluded our grasp.

20
Health and Hunger

I swung the gate closed after Pascal and his bicycle and whistled to Friday. Loping along the inside of the bougainvillea hedge, the dog pivoted in a flash and bounded back to me. Dust spurted from the lawn under her feet, and her lithe and shining body carved the early morning air into a kind of sculpture. I could see the title in a museum: Mammal in Flight.

A tall boy hung admiringly over the gate. "Your dog goes like an antelope. I've never seen a dog run like that."

"She is fast, isn't she?" I agreed. With that compliment to warm us, Friday and I made our little tour around the house and yard. She was ecstatic that it was not a teaching day for me. I should have been ecstatic, too, but I wasn't. I was restless. Now that the end of every week wasn't taken up with fever and chills and nausea, I had time—free time. Time to do something wonderful for somebody. That was it.

Here I was in Africa. Aside from my eight hours of teaching per week, I was making no contribution at all. It was embarrassing to compare myself to my friends. There were Pat and Earl, working in refugee camps in war-torn Vietnam. There was Janet, in VISTA in the heart of Philadelphia, tutoring and helping with food co-ops. There was Nancy, teaching disadvantaged children through a haze of daily fevers. And what about Susan? Susan was playing with her dog in the gardens of a lovely stone and stucco villa, while her servant was out buying rice and tomatoes for lunch. It was embarrassing.

Over the back wall I heard a loud tangle of Swahili voices, some laughter, and the steady pounding of corn in a mortar. Water ran splashing from a hidden faucet; the furious yells of a small child and the fragrance of soap told me that someone was getting a hairwash against his will. I could take that baby, I thought, and take care of him. I could make his little clothes and cook oatmeal for him.

But what was I thinking of? Listen here, Susan, I scolded. Does Africa need you or do you need Africa? The people next door seem to be doing fine without you. And, anyway, you didn't come to the Congo with a "call." Not that kind of call. You came for love. Don't lay on the Congolese the burden of making you feel needed.

I shrugged my shoulders and looked up the smooth gray trunk of the papaya tree. Under its cluster of leafy umbrellas was the yellowing underbelly of the ripest fruit. My mouth watered, and I looked around for the long pole I needed to coax it down with. Friday whined and romped around me as I took aim for just the right niche between the tree trunk and the softening fruit, gave a quick upward and outward thrust, then dropped the pole and ran to catch the flying papaya before it splattered its rich golden flesh all over the ground. In my hand, the papaya gave off a warm, indolent aroma of honeyed flowers, like the creamy frangipani petals I had slipped through on the way to the altar on my wedding day.

This smell, this bright morning, this instant of my

life should be enough, I thought. Why couldn't I be more content? Why couldn't I at least take satisfaction in my husband's usefulness? It only exaggerated our differences to realize that Robby was busier than ever right now. When we came back from Victoria Falls, a young man named Chipeng had moved down from Wembo Nyama with his four children and his nine nieces and nephews to become the new director of the social center. Robby was to gradually give Chipeng the responsibilities he himself had recently assumed, since it was only a matter of months until our departure.

Well, I could do one thing. I could go in and console myself with a slice of fresh papaya drenched in lemon juice. Twisting a hard green lemon from its leafy branch, I headed toward the house. Friday bounded ahead. Suddenly her ears flipped forward and her body tensed; in two seconds she was off like a flash to wait at the gate. Soon I heard the Peugeot purr of the car. Robby? What was Robby doing home at midmorning?

Robby was not alone. He got out of the car looking shorter than I'd ever seen him beside John and Jude, two of the English-speaking Sudanese students from the university. Like slender ebony tree trunks they were, incredibly tall and slender. I had never noticed them before. Their small, fine-shaped heads, charcoal-black with a suggestion of blue, seemed too heavy a burden for such frail stalks and on the verge of pulling their whole bodies over. Robby took them into the living room through the front door and then found me putting down the papaya and lemon in the kitchen.

"Home for coffee break?" I asked, surprised.

"More than that," he said hesitantly. "Do you have anything to eat?"

"Well, what do you mean?" I asked. "Is it your lunch you want? Pascal isn't even home from the market with it! Where did this big appetite come from all of a sudden?"

"No, I don't mean me," Robby said, quietly. "It's John and Jude. They haven't eaten in four days."

"What? I thought they ate at the university! I thought they were on a scholarship!"

"Evidently the university is closed for a week, and these students on a UN scholarship have neither money nor food for the interim. They came by my office this morning, very reluctantly, but they didn't know what else to do. When they inquired at the UN here, they were told their scholarship covered their education, but not maintenance. Now you tell me how someone with refugee status, who can't return to his home country, and who is a student in this country, is supposed to provide for his own "maintenance."

As he spoke I was pouring orange juice and rummaging in the cabinets for the box of dry Belgian biscuits. "We can talk about it later. They need something light in their stomachs right away." I sliced the still-warm papaya in half and scooped out the shiny black seeds while Robby got out a tray.

No wonder they looked so slender! As we sat together and talked in the living room, I was tongue-tied and awed by the dignity of their hunger, as if in the presence of death. How helpless and abandoned they must feel! First, war tearing into their comfortable upper-class life; expatriation; separation from family forever; then hope through a UN scholarship; and now, hunger and a feeling of nowhere to turn. How can hunger sneak up on an educated person, an upper-class traveler? Can a person starve who, like me, has sat on an international flight picking at Nordic smoked fish and marinated fennel and spreading French cheese on a crusty roll? What goes wrong?

Cooking had never been so rewarding as it was that morning. While John and Jude rested and ate slowly of the light snack, Pascal and I made soup and pudding with a passion, whipped up a meat loaf for a later supper, and peeled potatoes to be scalloped and baked with the meat loaf. John and Jude would eat today—and I, I need look no further for my creative project.

By Sunday afternoon, we were alone again. Our friends—thanks to Robby's persistent visits to the UN office in their behalf—had money for restaurant meals and were off on their own, looking a little more substantial and this-worldly than they had the day they came to us. I felt at peace and ready for anything, even the motorcycle which I usually viewed with suspicion.

"Come on, jump on behind me," Robby said. "There's a trail I want to follow."

The machine was popping smoothly after his little run to push-start it, and I settled myself on the seat behind him, my arms around his khaki-clad middle. We headed out through the wide deserted city streets, Sunday-afternoon siesta time wiping activity from them as a wet sponge wipes marks from a slate. It was a perfect late-summer day, and even the rainstorms were thinning out so that we might, with good luck, have sun the whole afternoon. In only a matter of a few blocks, we were passing the outskirts establishments, the Greek bakery where we bought our crusty *pistolets* for impromptu guests to munch with cheese and tomatoes, the butcher shops, the laundries, the junky car repair places ringed with barbed-wire fences. And then the tall elephant grass.

It was as if by permission of that grass that Lubumbashi existed at all—a giving way for only a matter of a few thousand meters. To such an expanse of grass that was a mere nothing, and the city's existence likewise. The pavement gave way to red ruts and a narrow path where many bare feet had padded and softened the harsh wheel marks into a smoothness fit for a child on his way to school, or a woman with a basin of market bananas on her head.

My mouth was two inches from Robby's ear. "Do you think we'll see any wild animals?" The elephant grass gave a person that feeling.

"Maybe a tiger!" he yelled back.

"There are no tigers in Africa!" I shouted in protest. "Tigers are in India!"

"There's one tiger in Africa!" Robby insisted. "It escaped last year from the zoo here in Lubumbashi! Keep an eye out for it!"

The path narrowed, or more accurately, the grass took a giant step toward us from each side, so that it lightly brushed my back or pulled at my hair as the motorcycle passed between. The sun darkened for a moment as we passed through a stand of tall evergreens, and then on the other side was a sunny ravine threaded by a milky stream.

While Robby stopped to determine the depth of the stream before fording it, I waved back to the women washing clothes a little way upstream. Wet, shiny dark hands played a satisfying, rhythmic slap-squash, slap-squash on a sudsy lump of cloth against a rock, and a banner of harmony wove itself through the limpid air as the women sang together. Drying wash was impaled on stiff grass heads like so many bright-colored butterflies mounted for display.

We churned through the shallow ford, while the

banner of song frayed and changed to friendly laughter at the two strangers getting their feet wet. Wet feet felt good. The afternoon sun was slapping color into our faces, and the transpiration of the thick grass on either side gave the impression of making our way through a steam bath.

"There's your wild animal!" Robby yelled as he swerved to miss a duck waddling down the middle of the road.

It was no tiger, that's for sure, nor did it resemble any duck I had ever seen. Shaped like a ferry boat, black and rugged, its white head sported a warty red growth and a black patch over one eye above the fiery orange bill. He looked like something you wouldn't want to meet in a dark alley and bore absolutely no resemblance whatsoever to the tiny balls of yellow fluff that were scattering into the grass. There was a village ahead.

"This is Chipopo," Robby called back over his shoulder, "where the Methodists have a church and a school." He drew up beside a tiny mud-brick building. "How would you like to teach here, Susan?" We got off the motorcycle to explore the deserted building. One mud wall had triangular chinks in it for ventilation, while the other wall was mostly door. The floor was swept earth. The only other features of the room were a small scratched blackboard on the front wall, three split log benches, and several shaky-looking stacks of mud bricks apparently used to support a slate for someone fortunate enough to own one. There wasn't a scrap of paper or a book to be seen anywhere.

"It makes my classroom in Lubumbashi look like a palace, doesn't it? I've got nice blackboards, plenty of chalk, smooth cement floors, windows with glass in them, tables, benches, and even some paperback English books the students can share." I had complained about *my* classroom atmosphere!

By this time a crowd of children had naturally gathered, but we were helpless to converse beyond the "Jambo!" stage. Frustrated, we turned and left, waving our good-byes to the little crowd of natural show-offs that were performing just for us and dissolving into giggles at their own antics.

The sun slipped behind a grove of crooked trees, and shadows lengthened with exaggerated tropical speed as we made our way through dirt paths in the direction of the city. Could one really get to a major city within minutes from where we were then? It seemed impossible as we slowly maneuvered past a crowd of dancers spilling out from under a gigantic mango tree. An alcoholic haze seemed to hover over the mellow crowd, and the drums beat languidly, with a pleasant fatigue as if winding down from a whole day of it.

"Smell the palm wine?" Robby asked over his shoulder. The evening breeze did have a fermented bite to it. I might have been passing an orchard where overripe peaches rotted on the ground, abuzz with glutted bees.

Darkness was soon deep and unbroken except for the thin light on the front of the motorcycle, which added menacing shadows to the towering grasses.

I think I was already braced for the blow when it came. There was a loud "Thwack!" and a gasp from Robby as he jerked back against me and brought the slow-moving cycle to a willing stop.

"What was it, Robby?" I cried.

He shook his head rapidly, snorted twice, and wiped his face with his left hand. His right hand he raised into the dim, wavering illumination of the headlight. There sat a small brown owl, just as stunned as we were by the encounter.

"Good I had my glasses on!" Robby muttered, spitting feathers between every other word. The owl blinked and looked as if he would have said a lot if he could, before suddenly lifting off Robby's raised hand and disappearing out of the thin circle of light.

"There's my wild animal encounter for the night," I said, giggling now that things weren't so threatening.

"Better to hit an owl at night than the only tiger at large on the African continent," Robby agreed, "but I'd better watch the road in front of me. Those birds sit there in the warm sand of the road after dark and can really catch you by surprise when they fly up in your face."

Something else caught me by surprise. A subtle ruddy glow over the rim of the horizon, and, immediately, a not-at-all-subtle blaze of a copper moon, low and molten as if thrown up just that moment from the smelting furnaces of the Gécomines refinery. To confirm that illusion, the familiar contours of the tall smokestack and the angular slag pile stood out black against the radiance of the rising moon. The copper moon gave shape and warmth to my world again, my African world, and Robby and I rode on into Lubumbashi on now-familiar ways. On a side street, the smell of potatoes in sizzling oil drew us to a tiny window in a wall marked *Friture.* The hot grease-spotted newspaper cone full of French fries warmed my hands the rest of the way home.

Several weeks later, Robby caught me out in the courtyard cutting the top off the rubber tree that threatened to climb right out of the courtyard and clamber over the roof. "Just wanted to warn you, sweetheart. The Wolfords, from Kapanga, will be staying here with their children the next day or two. Was it just last week you were wondering what you could do with yourself? Well, you've been running a rest home and guesthouse ever since."

It was true. We had had guests all along, but suddenly it was a full-time occupation. Was it in answer to my need to be needed? Before the month of March was half over, Robby figured I had already served seventy "person-meals" besides our own. By month's end, we had spent only three nights alone in our house. Among the people needing lodging were the chaplain from the University at Kisangani, several Paxmen on their way out of the country, our Mennonite Central Committee Director Ray Brubacher (who still claimed us in spite of Robby's un-Paxman-like marriage!), Methodist pilots, Dave and Mary Jo Schmidt from Mulungwishi, and the Horace Butlers, who were waiting to fly to South Africa for medical attention.

There were guests who shared Robby's interest in radios. Some—like Marv and Jean Wolford of Kapanga—had even depended on amateur radio to nurture their love affair—just as Robby and I had its crackling airwaves to thank that we were able to trust each other enough to plan a marriage long-distance.

"Yes," laughed Marv one evening as he and Jean and little three-year-old Andy sat at our table. "We entertained Jean's whole neighborhood back in the USA one evening. I don't remember what frequency we were using, but the next day Jean discovered that in the middle of the evening news, all of her neighbors were startled to lose Walter Cronkite's voice, and to hear instead, 'Oh, Marv, I miss you so much!' and 'Jean, darling, I love you and can't bear to be out here without you!' Jean had a hard time living that down."

The next afternoon, while Marv and Jean took care of business and shopping in Lubumbashi, Robby and I took care of little Andy. The golden head and big round inquisitive eyes made me think of how a son of Robby's could look. I was charmed by the child. Andy himself was charmed by our car and couldn't tear himself away when Robby chose that afternoon to adjust the points and plugs and work on the distributor.

Being a bit nervous about all that childish energy loose around the operation, Robby had a bright idea. Let Andy sit in the driver's seat and play with the controls on the dash. That should keep him safely confined and happy at the same time. While Andy made motor noises and swung on the steering wheel, Robby carefully loosened, removed, and arranged each tiny screw from the distributor on a flat place on the engine. As he leaned under the hood to remove the last screw, little Andy discovered the horn. What happened next was perfect slapstick comedy. At the loud blast of the horn in his ear, Robby jumped and fell onto the engine, his flailing arm swiping all the neatly arranged screws off their perch to rattle irretrievably down into the belly of the engine compartment.

"Well, Susan, I'm sorry!" laughed Marv that night after hearing the story. "By the look on Robb's face, I'm afraid we've ruined your chances of ever having children!"

21
Stalking the Crocodile

"There's a big one down there!" Ken shouted, and suddenly the horizon, the ground, and the air swirled together in a pinwheel of green, blue, and sunny yellow. I gripped the seat of the Cessna aircraft with one hand and Robby's hand with the other and tried to look straight ahead of me. The hand was cold and clammy, and I didn't dare glance at his gray face for fear of going over the edge of nausea myself, out of sympathy.

This was not a time to be sick. We were up and away from the city, and under the droning belly of the plane was passing the land of legend—the Congo.

"Watch her splashing in that waterhole!" said Ken, dipping the left wing and sailing downward with such a feeling of falling that I gasped. Like a giant insect aiming for a bite in that tough gray hide, the plane swooped over the annoyed elephant's back, turned and dipped and headed back for another look. This time she was ready for us. Her raised trunk shot water into the air, her gigantic leafy ears thrashed the air as if to shoo us away, and if the plane's engines weren't so loud, I'm sure we would have heard a thing or two from that open mouth.

Before my instant of panic at being so close to the ground grew into a real fear, Ken had pulled the plane smoothly into a climb and we were once again on the way to Kafakumba, leaving the elephant to her solitude. Besides Robby and me, Ken was carrying Dr. Bergwall, past president of Taylor University, who was to be speaker at the Methodist teachers' conference at the small village in the interior.

We were all charmed by the wild scenery, but underneath the pleasure was the chill thought: If we went down here, in this tall dim forest hung with vines, who would ever find us? The treetops were deceptively soft-looking from this height, but I knew that there would be no happy bouncing from one springy mound to the other, if we were to crash. We looked down on endless bamboo thickets, like unkept tufts of grass in a giant's lawn gone wild.

I felt a little easier when we were once again over a grassy plain studded with thorn trees, where antelope drifted lazily, like tiny leaves in a rippled pool. The ghost of a track winding through the plain comforted me. The track widened into a sudden village, round grass-roofed huts like movable playthings on the sienna surface of swept yards. For the sake of the children below, Ken dropped the plane and circled the village, dipping his wings in a salute to the gathering crowd of tiny stick figures.

We were once again over a dense forest when Ken announced, "Lake Kafakumba!" Ahead was a sheet of sparkling blue, five miles of lonesome lake crowded by forest, papyrus swamps, and rushes. There was one small opening, and the plane lost altitude over the lake to find that clearing where nestled Enright's house and the mud-brick huts for conference accommodations. The grass airstrip was a light green slash in the darker green of the jungle, rushing up to meet us, and then jolting the plane to a bone-shattering stop.

"Ken was just kidding, wasn't he, when he said watch out for crocodiles?" I asked Robby that first evening as we sat on the pier watching the silhouettes of birds circling in their last flights of the day.

"He was serious. The villagers have had a lot of problems with crocodiles in Lake Kafakumba, and they say there's a big one lurking in this part of the lake," he answered. "Better be alert. This isn't Lubumbashi, Susan, where the only animals you might see are chameleons and rats and maybe a squashed snake on the road to the university. There are enormous pythons in the woods around this lake, too. The skin we've got rolled out along the wall in our living room was bought here, you know, the one that's fifteen feet long and at least a foot wide."

"I'll watch out," I promised with an involuntary shiver.

Apparently motion sickness only happens to Robby as a passenger. At the rudder of a motorboat, he felt just fine. The rest of the week, he spent all possible moments skimming over the lake with a satisfying amount of motor noise, wending his way through papyrus swamps and acres of water lilies, or sitting in the rain fishing. On the east side, the lake penetrated the forest, marked by stumps and a growth something like cypress knees. It was a lonely and mysterious place to explore, the motor silenced, and only the push of the oars and the slap of ripples against the boat to momentarily disturb the kingfisher, a flash of indigo and orange against the dim water.

Robby had no lack of company. When the delegates arrived from all over Katanga for the conference,

231

Robby found that many of the African teachers had never before been in a motorboat. The empty surface of the lake beckoned and so did the promise of exhilarating speed. From that moment on, all Robby's spare moments were spent taking passengers on pleasure rides.

Besides the Congolese teachers representing a variety of regions, there were Swiss, Norwegian, Belgian, English, and Americans among the hundred participants at the conference. That made meal-planning a challenge, but Lorraine was undaunted. Though there was not a grocery store within a day's drive, she skillfully planned and directed the cooking for a hundred people for a week. Tubs of bananas and fragrant pineapple for fruit salad, leafy heaps of red-stemmed pigweed to be chopped and boiled for *lenga-lenga*, huge kettles of rice steaming, feathers flying for a little chicken to flavor the vegetable sauce—the kitchen was a busy place.

I was fascinated to watch the cooks prepare *ugali*, and that night I remarked to Robby, "Do you realize that some of the Conglese can't eat anything even so bland as macaroni and cheese? They're used to having *ugali* with sauce every day, so Lorraine has to have that on the menu at each meal." I must have forgotten for a moment just what country Kafakumba was in.

"Macaroni and cheese?" Robby looked at me for a moment. "Susan, did you ever smell aging cheese when you didn't know it was cheese you were smelling?"

I tried to follow his train of thought. "Well, yes, it can smell like dirty socks. You mean. . . ."

"I mean that macaroni and cheese is only bland to you because you're used to it. It may be totally disgusting to someone who's never had it."

After that I viewed the white enamel pans of *ugali* with a little more respect. It was the bread of the Congo—the hamburger bun, the toast, the pasta. With a pot of boiling water to throw the flour in and a wooden paddle to shape it up, *ugali* was as quick to cook as a microwave dinner, the fast food of the bush. Not only was it instant; it was also the ultimate labor-saving meal. A dozen people could feast on it and a palm oil sauce to dip the hand-formed balls in——with only two bowls and the assorted fingers to wash up afterward.

With two Congolese cooks in the kitchen, I wasn't much real help. But as Lorraine kept things moving without ever looking hurried or hassled, I found myself listening closely to the Swahili she spoke with her co-workers.

I was suddenly very interested in learning Swahili, but here it was, April, and in a couple of months we would leave the Congo. The time to have learned Swahili was six months ago, but then I was too busy being sick. What a waste, I thought impatiently. Would I ever have another chance? Meanwhile, the appealing rhythms of the kitchen talk burrowed into my mind.

One morning I turned sleepily to find an empty pillow beside me. I was instantly wide awake. Robby up before me? This was a new state of affairs. Through the window of the Enright's cottage, a mellow fire seemed to dart off every surface; the lake was blushing with sunrise.

I slipped into my clothes, determined to join Robby down at the dock. I certainly didn't want to sleep through this historic moment—my husband awake and full of energy at six in the morning! But as I quietly closed the front door behind me, I saw him

233

crouching on a high point of the lake shore. The dark rifle against his shoulder sent a shock through me. He was taking careful aim at what?

Then I saw it too, far out in the lake, a long narrow crocodile shape half submerged. At just that moment, the rifle cracked. There were ripples just short of the target, where the bullet ricocheted off the surface of the water. Robby took aim again. Again, the sharp report tore through the early morning hush. This time there were no ripples—a direct hit. I strained to see through the ruddy morning light the death throes of that old crocodile, the menace of Lake Kafakumba.

The long shape floated calmly on as before.

Robby turned and saw me standing there. He smiled a bit sheepishly and shook his head. "Well, the crocodile is still at large. That must have been a log washed out of the forest there across the lake."

It wasn't the first time Ken's gun had gone into action in behalf of the villagers, though usually with better results. Many a hunting story Ken told began with a need he saw, whether for food or for protection or both. Right there, between the Enright's lake house and the village a mile or so away, a man had been going along on a bicycle when an angry bull elephant caught him, tossed him up in a tree, pulled him back down, stomped him to death, and then buried the body under a pile of leaves and branches. Such an easily angered elephant, rejected from his troop, was a threat not only to lives. It could also destroy a farmer's field as an afternoon snack.

Robby put the gun away. There would be no crocodile steaks that day, and the women doing their laundry would have to keep a sharp eye about them as usual.

As the conference went on, there were lots of quiet

times—free time to absorb the calm and beauty of the isolated site. Wandering around in the afternoons, I could stop and watch the old man they called "The Last of the Iron Age." Day after day he worked over his small pile of hot charcoal with homemade tools and bellows made of animal skins, struggling to extract pure iron from a bit of rough ore. The acrid smoke in my nostrils and the heat reflecting against my face as the wrinkled old man patiently worked with his bit of the earth, reminded me that this was not a photograph in an anthropology magazine. It was not a display in a museum. This was a friend of Bwana Ken, who chose to do his work where we could watch.

Another afternoon some of us trailed into the forest behind a different artisan. The vines he selected to cut with his machete bled a special sap that he formed into bouncy rubber balls for us all. The group of teachers came out of the forest teasing and throwing the balls at each other.

A potter sat under a tree with his mound of gray clay, creating with his bare hands, crude tools, and bed of coals and ash a variety of little black pots and big water jugs with ornate stoppers.

"Here's one I made especially for you Americans!" The cheerful little man pointed to a recent production. I was startled to see the stopper decorated with a baseball cap. The potter was so proud of his attempt at reflecting American culture that I felt like a traitor preferring a crocodile motif to that of the baseball cap. I wondered if our own attempts to identify with another culture weren't just as ludicrous sometimes.

What did we have to offer these African artisans? I wondered. Our own hardware and dimestore culture featured cheap metal gadgets, bright plastic playthings destined for a quick journey to the garbage can, and china trinkets of no practical use. We could go ignorantly along, knowing nothing but how to count out the change in our pockets, while these men reached deep into the heart of nature to coax forth, with beautiful frugality, the essentials of life.

The last evening at Kafakumba, Robby and I went out for one last after-dinner walk by the lake. The path led through rushes and grasses down to a pool formed by the water's edge. A woman bent from the waist over the last of her day's washing, her wrap skirt damp from the lapping lake waters. We exchanged "Jambo's" and parted the grasses to move on. Suddenly Robby froze.

"There he is," he whispered under his breath, and then he shouted at the woman to get out of the water. Pointing at what looked like the same sort of half-submerged log he had shot at, Robby yelled the word for crocodile in every language he knew. The woman lost no time in swooping up her laundry and disappearing through the elephant grass.

We waited just long enough to be sure that indeed this "log" was "floating" purposefully in the opposite direction of the natural drift of the lake—straight toward the little laundry pool. Then we too were off and running to safety. Behind us, the seasoned old crocodile was probably grinning to himself as only a creature with extra rows of teeth and a mouth like a front-end loader can do. He was still king of Lake Kafakumba.

In the pearly gray promise of predawn that last Kafakumba morning, I sat beside Robby on the lake shore. The teachers, guests, workers, and staff were quietly making their way from the mud-brick cabins, voices low, to join the growing crowd. A dugout canoe whispered by in the light mist. It was Easter morning.

" 'Take, eat; this is my body. . . .' ' The bit of bread in my hand, the crust in the hand of the science teacher from Wembo Nyama, and the other symbolic pieces broken and scattered through the gathering seemed to glow with the first rays of the sun streaking through the forest on the other side of the lake. We who had broken the lump of *ugali* together, who had peeled bananas and buttered bread—we were one in belief and purpose. We were sisters, brothers, and this lake had welcomed us as to a family reunion at the home place.

Why did the communion service have to end, the splendid sunrise moment grow into everyday daylight, the moment of belonging and shared purpose fragment into the inevitable journeys alone? But then that was the purpose of symbols, I thought. This bread was not to be forgotten like yesterday's breakfast toast; it held the lingering goodness of the bread of life.

That afternoon we were circling over a runway again, but not in Lubumbashi nor the grass strip at Kafakumba. We were passing low over the wide, palm-lined streets and neatly arranged houses of the village of Kapanga, an hour's flight from Kafakumba. Ken and Lorraine were going to spoil us, I thought, with these extra side trips! But when I protested, Ken laughed. "Oh, it'll be worth it," he said. "We're going to get you hooked on Africa. You'll be back; you'll see."

"Will we, Robby?" I asked him when we were walking around Kapanga that afternoon. "Do you think you'd ever want to come back?"

"I've been here nearly three years now," he said,

shaking his head. "There are other things to be done. I'm just twenty-three years old; who knows what's ahead." He thought a moment. "I know one thing. I won't come back again unless I have a specific skill, a unique contribution that only I can make. I've enjoyed making airport runs, being chauffeur to the bishop, getting things through customs, reconciling account books, buying supplies for the women's classes. But I've put in my time with the sort of thing just anyone can do. What about you, Susan? Would you come back to Africa?"

I thought a moment. Robby and I had had a perfect situation to enjoy a year's honeymoon—no in-laws, no job worries, no housing problems. There were stories to hear, people to enjoy, novel experiences to share. But was real life supposed to be like this?

"I'm like you, I guess," I said. "If I come back again, I want to be involved for real. I want to know Swahili. I don't want to just be on the fringes of things, looking on."

Robby changed the subject. "Here's the hospital where Dr. Eschtruth operated on my hernia two years ago. He's on furlough right now."

"That's the time when I didn't hear from you for six weeks," I said reproachfully. "I didn't know if the mercenaries had gotten you or if you didn't love me any more. I wasn't sure which would be worse."

"Dr. Eschtruth took me back to his house to recuperate from surgery," Robby went on.

"Is that where you threw the kerosene lamp chimney across the room to get somebody's attention when the anesthetic wore off?" I asked, laughing.

"Yes, though I think the kerosene lamp chimney was the one thing I had sense enough not to throw. I threw everything else I could get my hands on. It's the same house where Glen woke up one night hearing the dogs making a big racket. He sat up in bed to see what was wrong when suddenly through the open window leaped one of the dogs. It bounced on the bed and out through the open window on the other side of the bed. Glen was about to lie back down and relax when the leopard that was chasing the dog bounced on the bed and out the window too in hot pursuit."

The Methodists had a lot of projects going at Kapanga, among them the hospital, schools, and the translating of the Bible into the language of the Lundas. The Mwant Yav David Tshombe, paramount chief of the Lunda tribe, was a member of the Methodist Church there in Kapanga. Services didn't start Sunday mornings until his tall, impressive person was seated up front on his leopard skin rug.

The Tshombe family had instituted many reforms in village government. There were building and sanitary regulations, scales placed in the fields so women could avoid waste by harvesting only the food they could use in a day, and a good educational system. Of course the Tshombes were most known for their brother Moise, the famous leader of the Katangese Secession of the early sixties and eventually prime minister of the whole country until ousted by Mobutu. There had been great mourning here the year before when Moise Tshombe died mysteriously in exile.

But the world of national politics seemed far away on a sleepy, sunny afternoon in Kapanga. As Robby and I walked out of the village into the trees and fields and tall elephant grass, I heard something strange.

"Watch," Robby said, pointing to some small boys crouching in the grass. They looked shy at seeing us, but after some giggles, they went back to their work.

239

Folding a long piece of grass into an accordion-shaped whistle, the tallest boy put the grass to his lips and blew hard several times.

"Look in the grass," Robby said.

Like children behind the Pied Piper, grasshoppers several inches long came hopping up to the whistler, enchanted by the imitation mating call. While the boy kept blowing on the grass, his friends seized the deluded grasshoppers and impaled them one by one on a stiff reed.

"They'll take them back home and roast them for the evening meal," Robby whispered in my ear as I watched, amazed.

Here at Kapanga for those several days, it was our turn to be the guests. The Wolfords and the Amstutzes shared their cozy homes with us and delicious meals. Harold was still talking about the adventure of flying his twin-engine Piper Aztec across the Atlantic and all the way to the Congo. I was glad to get a chance to see the beautiful plane, with its increased passenger and freight possibilities. The day Ken was going to fly us back to Lubumbashi in his Cessna 180, a little squall blew up. We didn't mind postponing our departure an hour or two, sharing a pitcher of lemonade in Elsie's kitchen.

The rain stopped as suddenly as it had begun, and the sun was just struggling out when the radio crackled with a few terse words. The new Piper Aztec, with twenty-some hours of Congo flying on its logbook, had met with disaster. Harold had been attempting a landing just after the storm, when a capricious crosswind whisked the plane across the slippery runway into the tall grass on the other side. The grass caught the wings, spun the plane around, and stripped off the landing gear. Now the wait would begin for replacement parts and painstaking repair. Once more the plane would be swift and efficient to carry the sick and injured to a hospital, or workers to jungle-bound outposts.

22
What Africa Chooses to Give to You

A low, rising growl caught my ear. I looked up from the English papers in my lap and shivered. But, listening, I heard only the weak snap of the small fire I had made in the fireplace to give an air of warmth and life to the lonely, black-tiled living room. I glanced at the dark windows, with their iron grillwork, and then at the fragile expanse of glass opening into the courtyard.

Another low, throaty growl seemed to echo off all the walls and come from nowhere in particular. Suddenly my wary eye caught a bit of movement, a flick of fur, spotted fur! My heart skipped a beat.

And then a black, sleek body tumbled out from behind the sofa, shaking a leopard tail in its jaws.

"Friday!" I scolded with relief. "No! Drop that leopard skin!"

Sheepishly, reluctantly, the dog gave up her shabby treasure, the dried and aging trophy of someone else's hunt, but still exuding the inflammatory smell of cat.

I shook out the crackling leopard skin, something Robby had found stashed away in a dusty office attic months before. There were a few more tufts of hair

242

missing, and the tail now dangled from the rest of the body by only a few shreds of atrophied hide.

"What will Robby say when he comes back tomorrow?" I reproached the dog.

At the word Robby she put her head down on her paws in utter dejection, the nut-brown eyebrows wrinkling in distress and guilt. I couldn't stand it.

"Here, Friday!" I called. In an instant she was beside me with her head in my lap. In her happiness, her warm wet tongue smeared a long inky semicircle across the exercise on the present progressive that happened to be on the top of the stack.

"Oh, Friday, I'm going to miss you!" I whispered into the clean doggy smell behind her floppy ears.

The "last things" had begun. It was Robby's last trip to Zambia for supplies. These were my last English papers to correct. We had seen the last of our friends and mentors, the Enrights, who left for furlough soon after our trip to Kafakumba. With the dubious help of a hand-operated black monster of a Singer sewing machine, I had sewn the lace around the neck of the last traveling dress for Eileen and little Lindy, dressed the last of the four dollies to match their mistress, and gathered twenty-five friends for a good-bye reception for them. At the airport, Ken had taken me aside. "Susan, you've got to see that Robby comes back to Africa. I mean that. He belongs out here."

A knock at the back garden door brought Friday to her feet and listening. Morgan. I wasn't annoyed any more when he insisted on using that door; it was Morgan's way. I was just glad he was alive. The week before he was moving office furniture and scraped his foot under a heavy desk. When blood poisoning set in, Robby got him to Dr. Karistianos, the mustached

Greek whom I had seen most often brandishing a needle full of quinine.

"How are you, Morgan?" I asked, when Friday and I got the back door open. I could hardly move without stumbling over my eager protector.

"Much better, thank you," he answered. "The swelling is gone. The fever is gone." He was still proud of his Northern Rhodesian English. "I know Robby is away, and I wanted to say that if anything is wrong, I am in my house. Please call me if you have any problems."

"Thank you very much, Morgan," I said, and meant it. "It's nice to know someone is nearby."

"Well, good night, then." As he started away, he turned back. "I was just wondering," he said, hesitantly. "My foot was very sick. If a man had a foot like mine, and he didn't have a doctor like Robby got for me, the man would just—the man would die, wouldn't he?"

"Yes," I said, "he could die. But you're fine now, Morgan. Everything will be all right."

"Yes, I know, for me, it's all right. But I was thinking about the others, the ones that don't have a doctor. . . . Well, good night." And Morgan was gone in the darkness.

The cold metal door clung to my fingers like a frost-covered ice tray. This is the Africa no one imagines, I thought. The crisp cold of a dry season night, the approach of winter. Lubumbashi's 4500-foot elevation made a fireplace fire welcome in the month of May. By day, the sun shone fiercely out of a deep blue sky, but its warming effect disappeared with the last glow of sunset. People who counted on that equatorial sun to warm them day after day were ill-equipped to warm themselves on these cold nights, with only

244

their lengths of cotton cloth to wrap their bodies against the chill. They called this the "death season." Last year at this time Pascal's eldest son died of smallpox, and this week the baby—his only other son—had been very sick as well. I was glad to share the muttering Greek and his hypodermic needle with yet another of our extended family and with Dr. Karistianos's help we hoped the big-eyed baby would once more smile shyly at me from his mother's back.

Two days later, Robby and I drove home from the airport at sunset, bone-tired. The travelers Robby had brought back from Zambia were on their way again, and I looked ahead to the first quiet evening the two of us had shared in weeks. What had happened to all those empty days I had worried about filling creatively? I really didn't miss them, I thought happily, but I would enjoy curling up with a good book.

I wondered if among the dusty titles in Bishop Booth's bookshelves I'd find anything more arresting than ancient theological tomes and tattered Grace Livingstone Hill novels. Those raven-haired, high-minded heroes that had thrilled me at the age of thirteen somehow seemed insipid compared to the slight, half-blond bundle of energy I was sharing my days and nights with now. Maybe I could find a biography to read; even the poorly written biographies were interesting, just as lives could be interesting even when poorly lived.

As we pulled up to our driveway, we were surprised to find the wide, spiked gate standing open, and a friend from Mulungwishi standing in the yard petting Friday.

"I brought you someone for a few days," he said casually as we got out of the car. "I couldn't think of anyone else who had room. And I know Robby always likes to have first chance at overnight guests!"

Oh, not tonight, I thought to myself. Overnight guests mean dinner, and I wasn't planning anything for dinner. The vision of enjoying a readable biography began fading fast away. And then I saw the thin girl leaning against the backseat of the car with her eyes closed.

"She's from the secondary school at Mulungwishi," our friend went on, "and she has an abscessed tooth. She's supposed to see a dentist tomorrow morning and may need to stay several days."

Several days? But she didn't speak English; most of our guests spoke English! I thought wildly. What if she didn't like our food?

But Robby was already welcoming Ekoko Régine. "You're fourteen years old?" he asked. "Susan and I both have sisters who are about that age. It'll be great to have somebody around to tease again!" Régine managed a coquettish smile in spite of her swollen mouth, and suddenly I was happy we had this new guest.

Her oversized pajamas smelled fresh of strong soap, and she curled up in a chair watching me tuck in the corners of the blue Congo-made sheets. Aspirin had already numbed the pain of the abscess.

The door opened, and in came Robby with a bowl of Sunday evening popcorn and a pot of tea.

"Popcorn!" I gasped. "Popcorn may not be so good for an abscessed tooth, you know."

"Oh, it can't hurt her if she wants to eat it," Robby shrugged. "It's just a little starch. Come on, Régine, try it!" She didn't need a second invitation.

Hurrying home from school the next day, I felt a flutter of anticipation. Régine was there! We had a little sister to pamper.

But pampering was out of the question. She was already feeling better after the morning's visit to the dentist and was full of questions and ideas. I was surprised how naturally it came to share the French language as well as our soup and salad at lunchtime. Friday lay protectively by her bed when she took a nap, as if to claim her by adoption into the family.

Whatever I did in the kitchen, Régine was at my shoulder, peering and asking questions. Together we baked bread and cinnamon rolls. When I made a beef stew for dinner, she was all eyes.

"Could you please write down the recipe for me?" she begged. "And for the cookies you made?"

"Of course!" I said. "But maybe you have a recipe you can share with me. Let's trade!"

So the two of us sat at the kitchen table with a French dictionary and a Betty Crocker cookbook, laughing over our attempts at recipe grammar. "Beef Stew" and "Snickerdoodles" traded places with "*Sauce d'Avocats.*"

"So, you puree the avocados, add some chopped tomato and onion, add some salt, and lemon juice. That's it?"

"Let me show you," said Régine. And she whisked around the kitchen in an amazingly skillful manner for a girl who grew up as a part of an Otetela family in the African bush and was spending her school years in a spartan dormitory. I couldn't imagine doing the same at her age.

Régine's daily visits to the dentist were having the desired effect, and by the end of the week she was totally well.

"They're coming this afternoon to take me back to Mulungwishi," she said on Friday.

"Oh, you can't stay for the weekend?" I felt a sense

247

of dismay that our young guest was going to be on her way, as suddenly as she had come. But of course she had to go when they came for her. "We'll miss you," I said. I thought of my own sisters, and my heart sank to realize that even when I went back to Virginia, we'd never be living in the same house again, just being sisters.

I went into the bright corner room where Régine was packing her belongings. Under her neatly folded wrap skirts I slipped a gaily wrapped package. It was a trousseau slip, a rich lime green, knee-deep in frothy lace. This was one I had left in Lubumbashi while we went on our honeymoon, and the car thieves didn't get a chance at it. How much better it will look against her velvet brown skin, I thought, than against my pallid whiteness.

It was a week later, when a car from Mulungwishi drove into our yard again. "Here you go, Ackermans!" Our friend handed us a faintly warm, soft package. Then he reached into the backseat for what I first thought was a big club when he swung it about his head. But, no, it was a huge green and white striped crookneck squash.

"Who is sending us these presents?" I asked, puzzled.

"Your little house guest—Ekoko Régine," he answered.

So she wasn't content just to be our "angel unaware." I pulled back the paper that carefully covered a moist, fragrant loaf cake. Of course, the students had their gardens, so the origin of the welcome squash was no mystery. It would be great in a batch of "pumpkin pies." But where, in a bare dormitory, would Régine find what she needed to put together a delicious cake to arrive fresh for Robby and me, hours away? And who translated that recipe? And who taught her how to swirl the chocolate and the white batter together to make a marbled effect?

For days I thought about those two gifts with a warm glow. It was as if Africa herself had reached out to me with a pat on the hand and said, "I like you. You're special." Forget the hours of standing before an English class. Forget the medical help, the gifts of food and clothes. Forget the driving, the bookkeeping, the hospitality. Remember the bright green squash and the fragrant brown cake. Because it's not what you can bring to Africa, after all. It's what Africa chooses to give to you.

23
Persistently Africa

Robby looked up from the corner of the patio where he sat on a carved wooden folding chair, a forty-four pound elephant tusk supported upright between his knees. Dropping the file he was holding and leaning back to stretch, he asked, "Do you think this'll pass as worked ivory?"

Ken had given us the tusk before he left, a gift he had received many years before from a hunting village. He gave us, too, the warning that only worked ivory could be legally taken out of the country. Robby and I were not interested in a hundred ivory bracelets or a fancy carved tusk. Twice cheated out of our elephant carvings, all we really wanted was just this mighty tusk in all its naked glory. Did working include filing off the gray crust of dust embedded in this gigantic digging tool? We would find out. The mellow whiteness of the ivory itself was all the beautifying it needed for us.

The coals were just right, so I laid two small pieces of meat on the grill. "Do you realize this is the first time we've grilled steaks for two in our entire marriage?" I said happily. "I think we were waiting until all the ferns were as big as the rubber tree." I pointed to the ferns tumbling over the rocks at one side of the grass plot. "You've created a miniature botanical garden, with eight fern varieties!"

"Maybe we were waiting for an evening without any guests," Robby said, going back to filing the tusk.

I set the outdoor table with a square of black-and-white wax-print cloth. Into a low bowl I tucked a couple of creamy white gardenias from the front lawn and a blazing red hibiscus for love, even though I knew the hibiscus would curl up into a shy nothing within minutes. The bruised white plastic of our dishes somehow did not match my mood, so I laid out two wooden serving plates we had bought on our honeymoon, risking the grooves a knife would make.

The stars were near and bright in the fresh night air. "Why don't we sleep out here tonight?" Robby suggested as we sat down to our salad. "I could drape a mosquito netting over the clothesline, like we did that other time."

I burst into giggles. "And be surprised early in the morning by a couple of Paxmen who had come in on the night train? Like happened to us the last time?"

"Well, what's wrong with that?" Robby asked, in mock surprise. "Lots of people sleep outside with their whole families, here in the Congo."

"I don't know. It just seemed to flaunt your non-Paxman status, that's all."

"Hey, I enjoy my status!" Robby threw back over his shoulder as he went to remove the meat from the grill. The smell was mouth-watering.

My knife was poised over my browned steak when I heard the gate clang. "Robby, somebody's here."

"This was too good to last," he sighed, putting down his knife and fork before getting the first bite. I, not so easily dissuaded, popped a small piece into my mouth before following him to the door.

Anticipating our departure in a couple of weeks, we

had given away most of our house plants, cushions, statues, and water pots. But we still had sheets enough to offer hospitality to strangers, and that night the taxi from the airport brought us an American named Gary, who would be in town for several days. It wasn't the first time we had stretched a dinner meant for two, but the romance of the evening was broken. What was worse, Robby's three years of dealing with Congolese bureaucracy and city theft showed up in an unflattering way against our new arrival's innocent pleasure at seeing his African brothers for the first time.

The conversation was awkward. Gary was shocked to hear stories of theft, break-ins, and clever deceit that Robby had to tell. Our guest was convinced that in any situation, the American must be the aggressor and the African the victim. Robby felt that Africans were human beings not a great deal different from human beings anywhere, and that people everywhere sometimes take advantage of each other. While all the stories he told were true, I thought that he was being selective, choosing only the sensational and the shocking. I became uncomfortable enough that I went out on the street to give Friday a bedtime stroll.

Gary was a polite guest. On Sunday afternoon, he generously offered to take us out to dinner. This was something our guests often did—in retrospect, I'm sure it had something to do with the size of a serving of four-egg omelet when divided among five people. With Lubumbashi's international choice of restaurants, the menu could be Indonesian *nasi goreng*, Moroccan *couscous*, stuffed grape leaves beside a plate of *moussaka*, or a pepper steak followed by a whipped cream and ice cream concoction called a *dame blanche*.

252

Gary's choice that afternoon was a Greek restaurant whose menu was elegantly French. The waiter brought chilled plates of asparagus *vinaigrette*, followed by *caneton à l'orange*, half a tiny duckling in orange sauce garnished with deep-fried potatoes in the shape of hickory nuts. Robby and Gary were getting along fine today, thank goodness, I thought. Robby's love for others was not so skillfully hidden as it had been the night before, and Gary was asking questions and willing to listen to answers. A lovely apricot *tarte* finished off the meal, and then we went home, looking forward to a relaxing Sunday afternoon nap before the evening church service.

I paused in the courtyard. "Gary, thanks; that was a meal to remember."

Then I opened my bedroom door and gasped. Every dresser drawer had been jerked open or flung to the floor; the two closet doors were standing out at full tilt; even the mattress and pillows of the bed had been shoved askew. Robby and I had given away all our clothing except thirteen pounds each, in anticipation of traveling home. Looking over the ransacked room, I couldn't believe that two times thirteen pounds of clothing could make such a mess when flung all over the floor. My little Venetian painted-leather purse was lying next to my foot. In a daze, I picked it up. Every compartment had been ripped open, but the small change amounting to about a dollar—the remnant of my week's spending money—was all there.

I turned to Robby, who had followed me in. "What did they want? They left my money!"

"They wanted real money—not your small change. Susan, the passports! The camera!" Those were the only valuables we had left. The radio had been stolen long ago and of course there were no jewels.

We rushed into the adjacent study only to find more of the same havoc. All the paper supplies had been flung out of the writing desk, Robby's briefcase opened and dumped. Standing ajar was the door of the small cabinet built into the bookshelves, the place we had chosen to store the passports and camera. Breathing a prayer, we looked inside.

"They're there!" Robby whispered.

"That's wonderful!" I answered thankfully.

Then Gary burst in.

"I've been robbed!" he shouted. "I think my camera's gone! They took my traveler's checks!"

On closer investigation, we located Gary's camera unharmed in a corner of his room. It appeared that Gary was missing only his traveler's checks, which had not been countersigned and thus could be replaced. A packet of money worth about forty dollars, my salary for a month's teaching, was missing from the desk. But we were still amazed and thankful that the camera and passports were safe.

"The thief must have heard the car in the driveway," Robby conjectured, "just at the moment he was opening this cabinet. Since he had to get back over the courtyard wall before we got into the house, he probably just ran with the money and traveler's checks he already had."

A heavy footprint in the moist grass on the other side of the wall confirmed our theory of an over-the-wall-into-the-courtyard entry.

Gary was upset and couldn't understand our calmness. "You mean you didn't lock your doors?" he asked. "The thief just walked in from the courtyard!"

"We lock the outside doors," Robby explained. "But since there's an inner door in the courtyard leading to each room, it was a big inconvenience to lock and unlock each one every time we left the house. Besides," he went on, glancing at me with eyes full of mischief, "it would be a shame to be so suspicious of the Congolese."

"Well, anyway, aren't you going to call the police?" Gary insisted. "Someone just goes through all your belongings and takes my travelers checks; you've got to do something."

I had a feeling of déjà vu. There I was, standing in a state of shock before the empty place in the yard where our Dodge Dart was supposed to be, wondering why somebody didn't call the police. I smiled to myself, a smile that probably only bewildered Gary the more. The last twelve months had certainly been educational.

Robby said soothingly, "We've lost your traveler's checks, which we can go to the bank and replace tomorrow morning, and Susan's forty dollars worth of zaires. Even if the police ever found the thief, which is highly unlikely, the money would already have been spent. We'd never get that back, and there would probably be expenses involved in prosecuting the thief, so we only stand to lose the more by bringing the police into it."

By the look on Gary's face, I could tell that the foundations of his existence were being shaken.

"Don't worry. I'll certainly report it to the police during working hours tomorrow. Of course they should know about it, but I'm not looking to them for any help in getting stolen goods back. Now, how about a good game of Scrabble! Chinese checkers? Kangaroo Chinese checkers?"

On the list of last things, there comes inevitably the last morning. Walking outside in the chill of sunrise to harvest my last papaya, I knew that as happy as we had been here on Avenue Maniema, I could say good-bye to the bare, cold house without a tear. I could look ahead with delight to the tiny student apartment Robby and I would probably share next year, tucking this nine months in our stone-and-stucco villa into memory's album beside the flower-hung honeymoon cottage of the Vanhees.

But the living things—the people we knew, the dog who loved and trusted us, even the trees and the flowers we had cared for—made good-bye a painful word. I cradled the night-chilled ripeness of the golden-green papaya in my hands and looked up the leafy-topped tree trunk for the last time. Tomorrow's fruit would fall into someone else's hands. I heard Pascal rattling pans in the kitchen, and with a pang, knew that my next kitchen, however cozy, would lack the dignity and presence of this man we had come to depend on and to respect.

"Pascal, I want to take your picture!" I said, going in with my greetings and my papaya. "When we have children, we'll tell them all about you."

Though I would rather have had a picture of him in his apron, chuckling over some of Robby's impossible stories, he would have none of that. Taking his sport coat out of a closet, he removed the apron along with his smile and took a solemn position by the fern garden. Even Robby, stepping out into the morning with a suitcase in hand, could not bring a smile to his face. But after all, it was Pascal's face, I thought, not ours. I snapped the picture.

"There!" I said, trying to be lighthearted. "We'll always have this to remember you by."

As Pascal turned back to the kitchen, I was surprised by the shadow that passed over his face. Why,

Pascal is going to miss us, too, I thought.

It would have been impossible to take a good photograph of Friday that morning. She was a blur of anxiety. It wrenched my heart to see her pain, and the sooner we delivered her to her next owner, the better. A new volunteer named Paul was to keep Friday until Dr. Eschtruth came back from furlough and took the dog to Kapanga with him.

Paul was also going to inherit the motorcycle, so that morning he walked over to pick it up. We chatted a while, and Robby gave the trusty machine one last pat. Then Paul revved up the engine and headed for the gate I was holding open. Just then around the corner of the house came a little black whirlwind in a cloud of dust. Before Paul could go the few yards to the gate, a frantic Friday had hurled herself through the air at the moving motorcycle. Over went the motorcycle, sprawling in the gravel of the driveway with its wheels still spinning helplessly like a flipped-over roach waving futile legs. Paul hit the dust, too, luckily at some distance from the heavy machine. Friday stood fiercely over the fallen machine, panting but determined. There was only one person in the world who could leave the yard on that motorcycle, and that person was Robby.

"Hey, fella," Robby said soothingly, after the first moment of surprise. He put his arms around her neck. To Paul, who was blinking and dusting himself off, Robby was apologetic. "Maybe I'd better drive this out of here for you. Are you okay?"

"I'm fine," Paul answered. "But, yes, maybe you'd better drive it out, so Friday won't be confused about being a guard dog."

"You won't change your mind about taking care of her for the next few weeks, will you?" I asked, wondering how long Friday would keep him filed away in the category of motorcycle thief.

"No, I'll give it a try. She's a smart dog. She'll know when you're gone for good."

Our flight was scheduled to depart in the late afternoon. It was unreal to be taking the familiar highway to the airport, knowing that today it was only a one-way trip. The check-in desk for Air Zaire was a scene of bedlam.

"Why is everyone pushing and yelling?" I asked Robby.

"This is normal," he answered, though his expression betrayed his own concern. "This time of year you have a lot of Europeans trying to go on vacation, and this flight only happens twice a week. Don't worry; we've had reservations for weeks. I'll try to get in line and get our suitcases weighed."

I sat down on my attaché case in the crowded hall. A magnificent Congolese woman in gold brocade made her way through to the ticket counter, the crowd falling back before her. Oh, to be a princess in one's own country, I thought, feeling pale and humble and uncertain on my precarious perch. A tangle of Greek merchants came through pushing huge metal trunks, padlocked and ready to go. A comradely knot of Belgian schoolteachers, the women in miniskirts and the men in tight tapered trousers and shiny shoes, smoked away their waiting time. A French family kept track of a toddler on a leash, a poodle in a traveling cage, and heaps of bulging hand luggage. We'll never all get on one little airplane, I thought.

Robby was back, shaking his head. "I can't believe it, but our name has been taken off the passenger list. I should be able to believe it, after three years here, shouldn't I? I think they just way overbooked this flight."

The scene at the check-in counter had become a roaring free-for-all. Only a scant majority of the passengers had been awarded seats, and some of the rejected ones seemed to be ready to take it to the president.

"They said that it's possible another plane will come in from Kinshasa later on tonight," Robby said, "but I've never known it to happen."

"What shall we do?" I asked. It was inconceivable that having said our good-byes, we would creep back to a place that had already closed in after us, like the waters from which a gasping fish had been taken. Just as Africa had impassively accepted our arrival, it already believed in our departure. So must we.

"We'll stay right here at the airport," Robby said. "We'll be on the next flight whenever it is."

Sunset came and went. The long, slim DC-8 on the runway swallowed a great gulp of the crowd and roared up into the darkness. The way people had been yelling and gesturing, it was difficult, but hilarious, to imagine them seat-belted into the aircraft next to each other, listening politely to the stewardess's safety instructions.

Hours passed. What was left of the crowd thinned out toward midnight. Robby and I sat together on the chilled concrete beside the fenced runway. The African night was flower-sweet, and spiced with a hint of dry-season dust in the air. It teased me with little rushes of wind through the knit of my Irish sweater. The fragment of a moon was climbing up the sky as if late to school, paling as it went. We were quiet, like interplanetary travelers put to sleep for the voyage that would take them from one world to the next.

Suddenly we were dazzled by two powerful landing lights cutting a swath through the darkness from heaven to earth. With the throb and whine of mighty engines, a huge jet touched down and thundered toward the terminal.

"It's an American airline! It's Pan Am!" Robby was on his feet and shouting. "Pan Am doesn't *fly* to Lubumbashi!" His eyes were shining. "That's the first bit of the USA I've seen in three years!"

At this hour of the night, the customs and immigration people were too tired to play games, and we were soon boarding the surprise aircraft, marveling that we were "home." Were the casual blond stewardesses really chewing gum, or did it just seem to go with their American accents? They hung around the door, teasing the steward, welcoming the passengers in English, passing out *U.S. News and World Report* and the *Herald Tribune.* I smelled coffee.

"This is how it all started," I whispered to Robby as we made ourselves comfortable in our seats. "Only I was by myself."

"I like it better this way," he said, grinning like a kid with a new toy, arranging his briefcase just right at his feet and raising the armrest so I could lean against him.

We were airborne then and hurtled north in the dark of the wee, small hours. I pressed my face against the window glass to somehow get a feel for what I was leaving, not expecting to see anything below. But craters of a creeping, glowing red opened up here and there in the world spread below me. Grass fires, I thought to myself. The dry season burning of the fields. I could even smell a faint trace of smoke in the air of the cabin. In this small piece of flying America, the air we breathed was persistently Africa.

The moon was faltering in the sky, a far white fragment, a distant European relation to the robust copper ones I had known. In the morning there would be a hotel with flowered wallpaper and circular stairs. There would be lace curtains against a busy Paris street. There would be coffee and croissants on a marble-topped table.

"We'll have to go back, you know," I said suddenly to Robby.

"Go back? Why?" It was the farthest thing from his mind.

"To see if we can find another dusty old elephant at Victoria Falls," I said. "Maybe the third time will be the charm."

"Don't count on it," he laughed. "In any case, we still have the three-armed fetish that no one wanted to steal."

I smiled at him, but kept my deeper thoughts to myself. These twelve months in Africa had been as an unintended stop in an inn on my way somewhere else. Perhaps another year it would be my destination.

The Author

Since the wedding described in *Copper Moons*, Susan has divided her time between the old gray Yoder farmhouse in Denbigh, Virginia, and more adventurous years with Robby in Central and West Africa. Three young children, a bottle-fed bushbuck, a monkey, and numerous peace corps volunteers added immeasurably to the family drama of those years.

Susan attended Eastern Mennonite College and earned a B.A. in English from the College of William and Mary. She has taught in elementary, middle, and high schools in Newport News, Va., in Zaire, and in North Carolina. Her most challenging teaching experience was home-schooling her own children, Ilse, Hans, and Anje, in the isolation of the Zairian bush and in the dust and heat of the Mauritanian desert.

Today Susan teaches French in her home community of Denbigh, Va., where she lives with Robby and their three children. Her free-lance articles and stories for children have been published in magazines at home and abroad. In her home church, Warwick River Mennonite, she is involved in ministry to youth and children.